Some of the Whimsical Patterns that can be found Inside

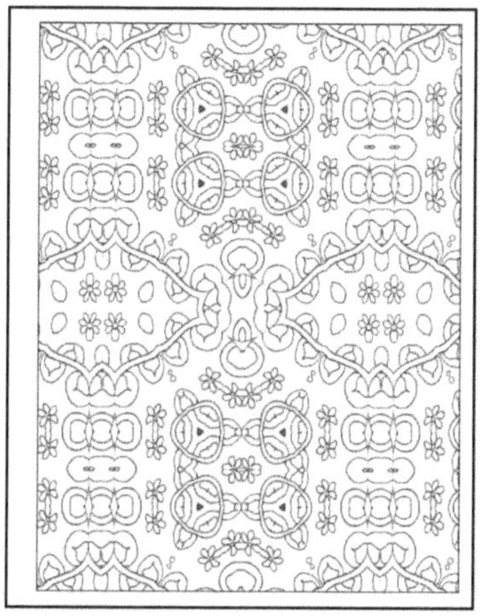

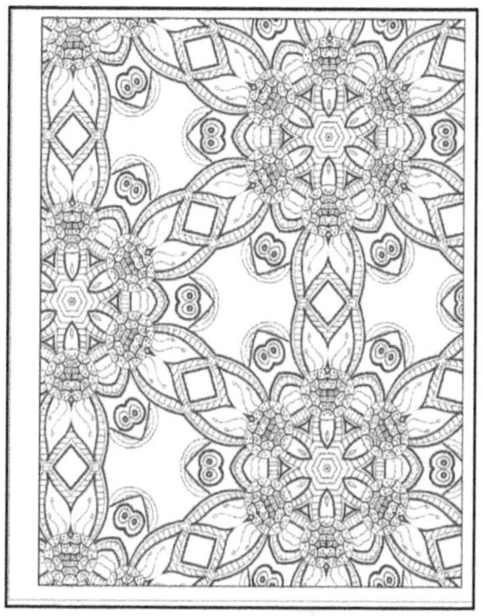

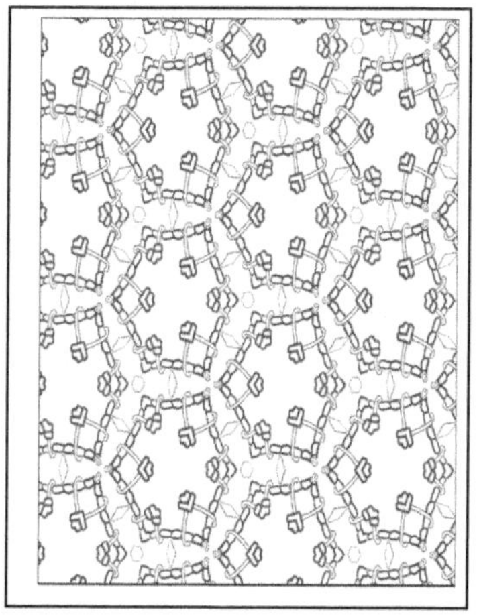

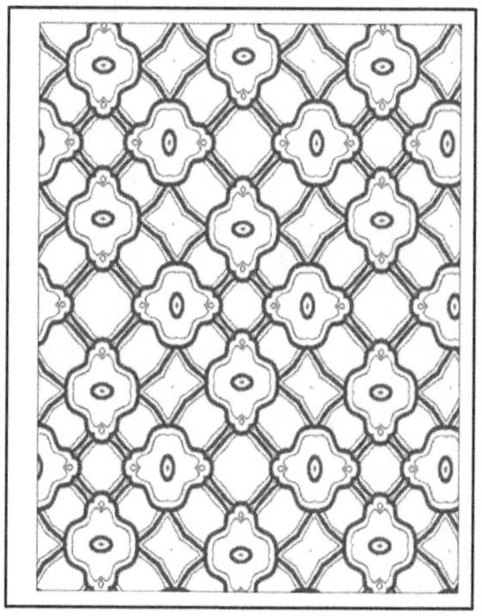

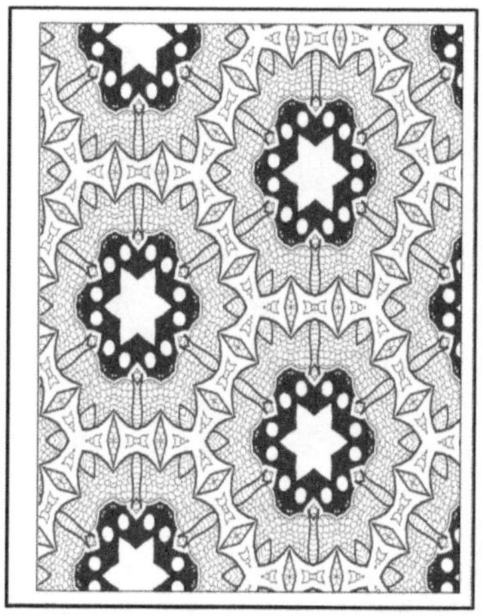

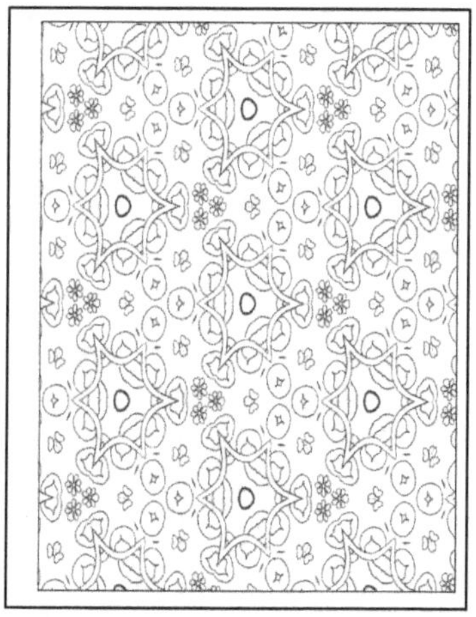

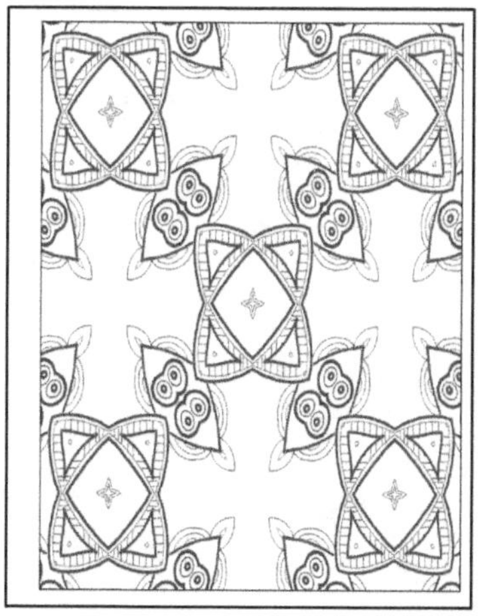

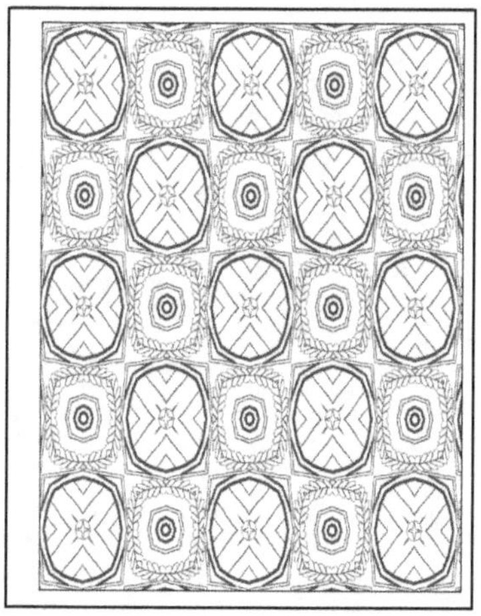

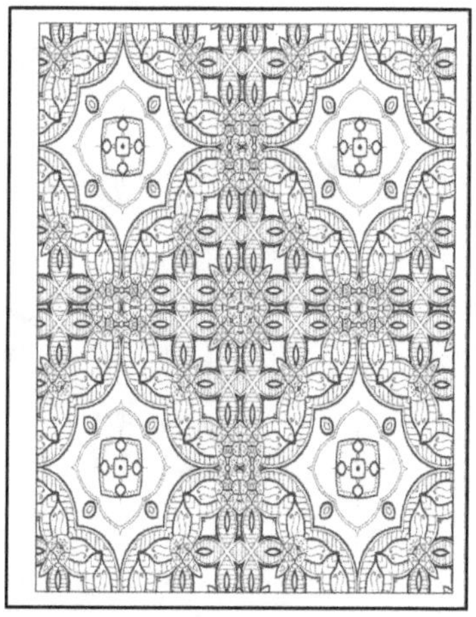

Visit my website at http://www.coffeeandcoloring.com

View my Etsy shop at http://www.artbyericah.etsy.com

Like my page on Facebook http://www.facebook.com/coffeeandcoloring

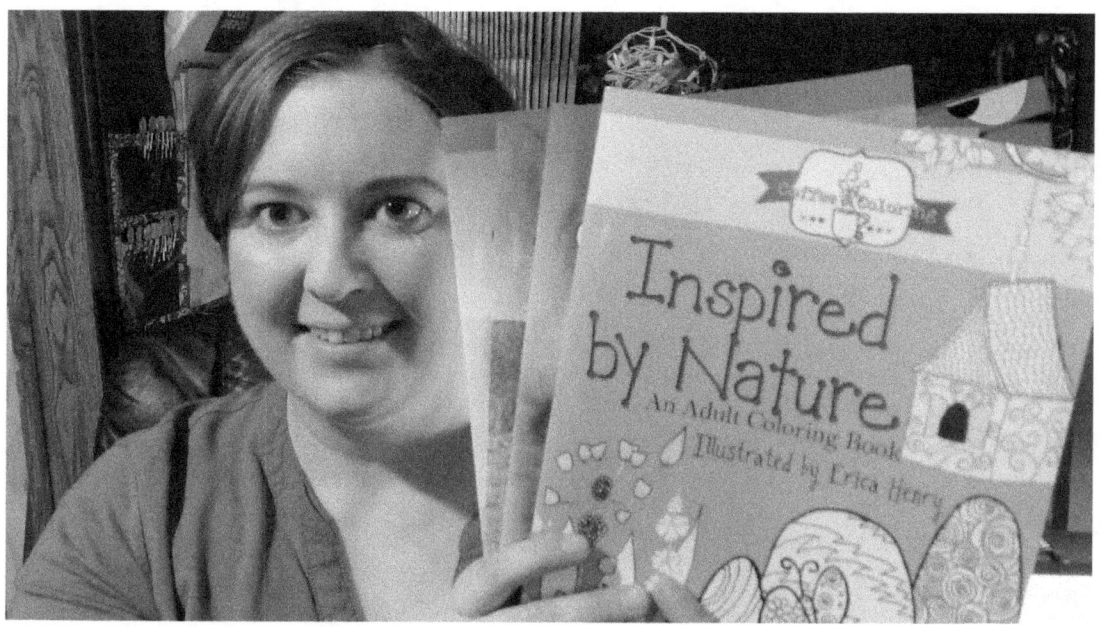

Hi there. My name is Erica Henry and I am the illustrator of the *Whimsical Pattern Series*. I'm so glad that you decided to purchase a copy of my book. I have spent hours hand drawing each of these designs for you, and now it is your turn to grab your art supplies and turn them into your own creations.

I have included some blank pages in this book so you can take them out and use them as a protection page as a precautionary measure to prevent bleed through when using markers or gel pens.

Please visit my website at http://www.coffeeandcoloring.com and say hi. I also have tutorials there as well. I love to see your coloring pages that you've done so please post them to Facebook page http://www.facebook.com/coffeeandcoloring.

I hope you are as excited to start this coloring journey, as I was to create the book. Now, grab your coloring supplies and get to coloring

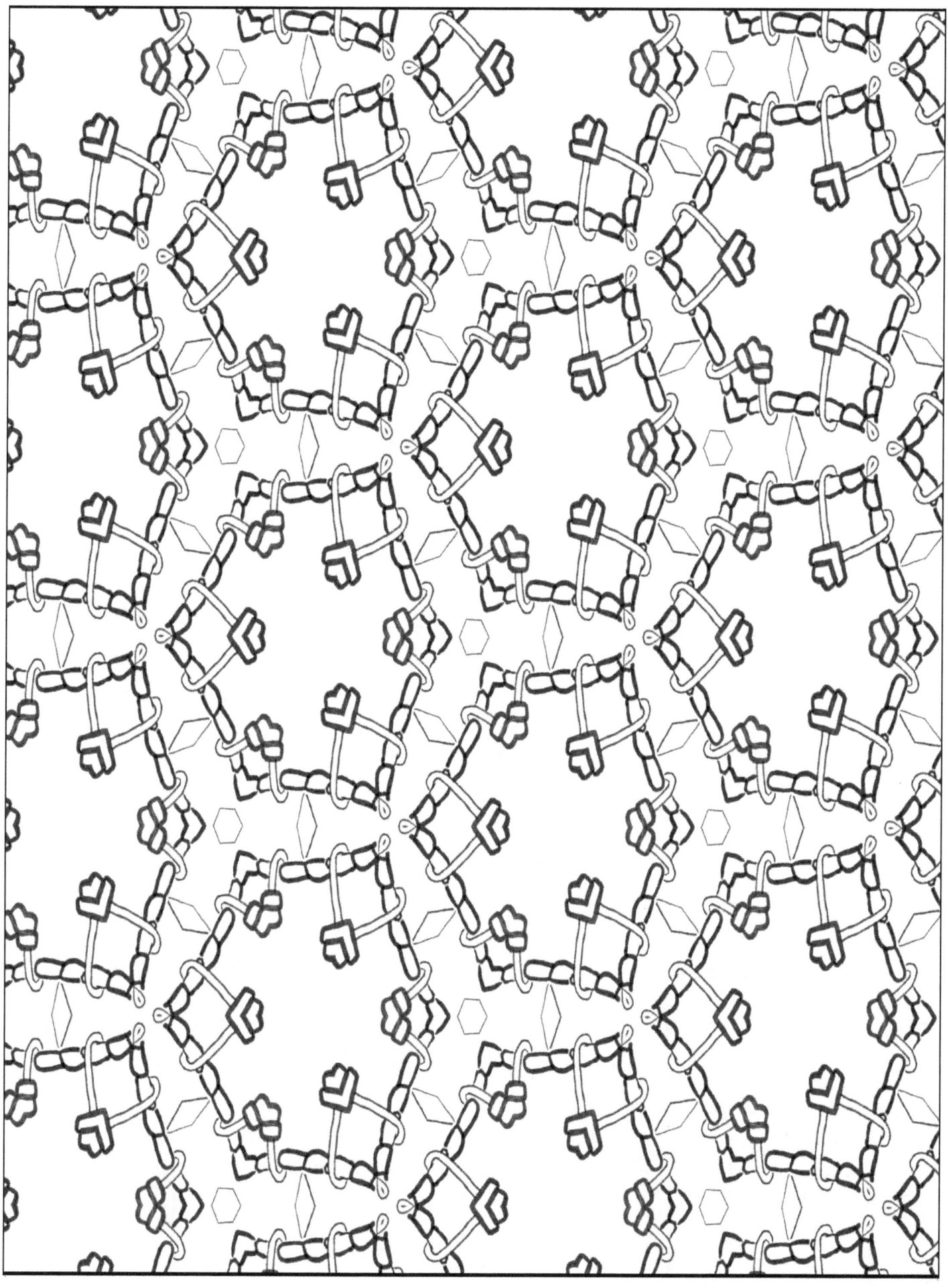

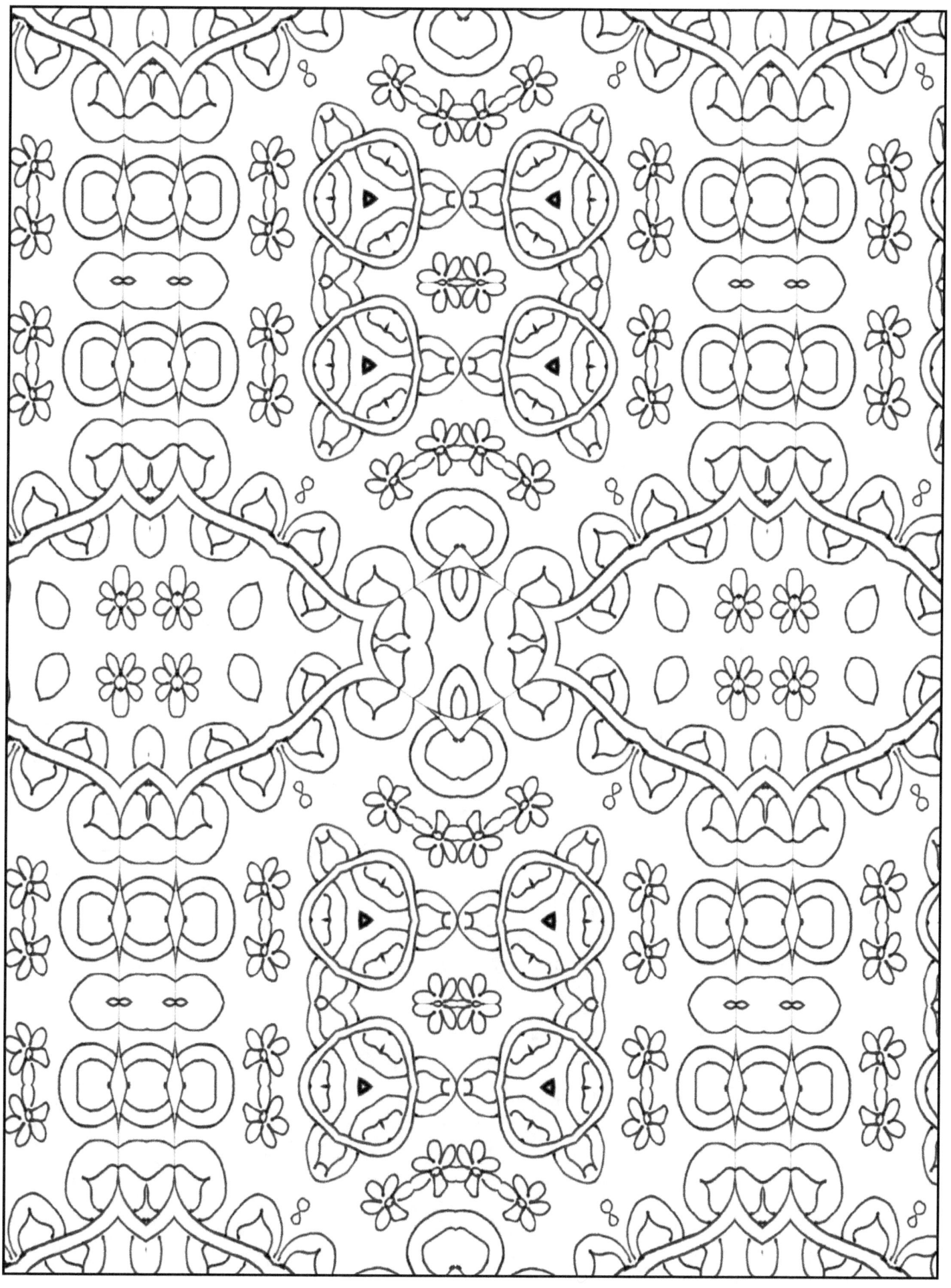

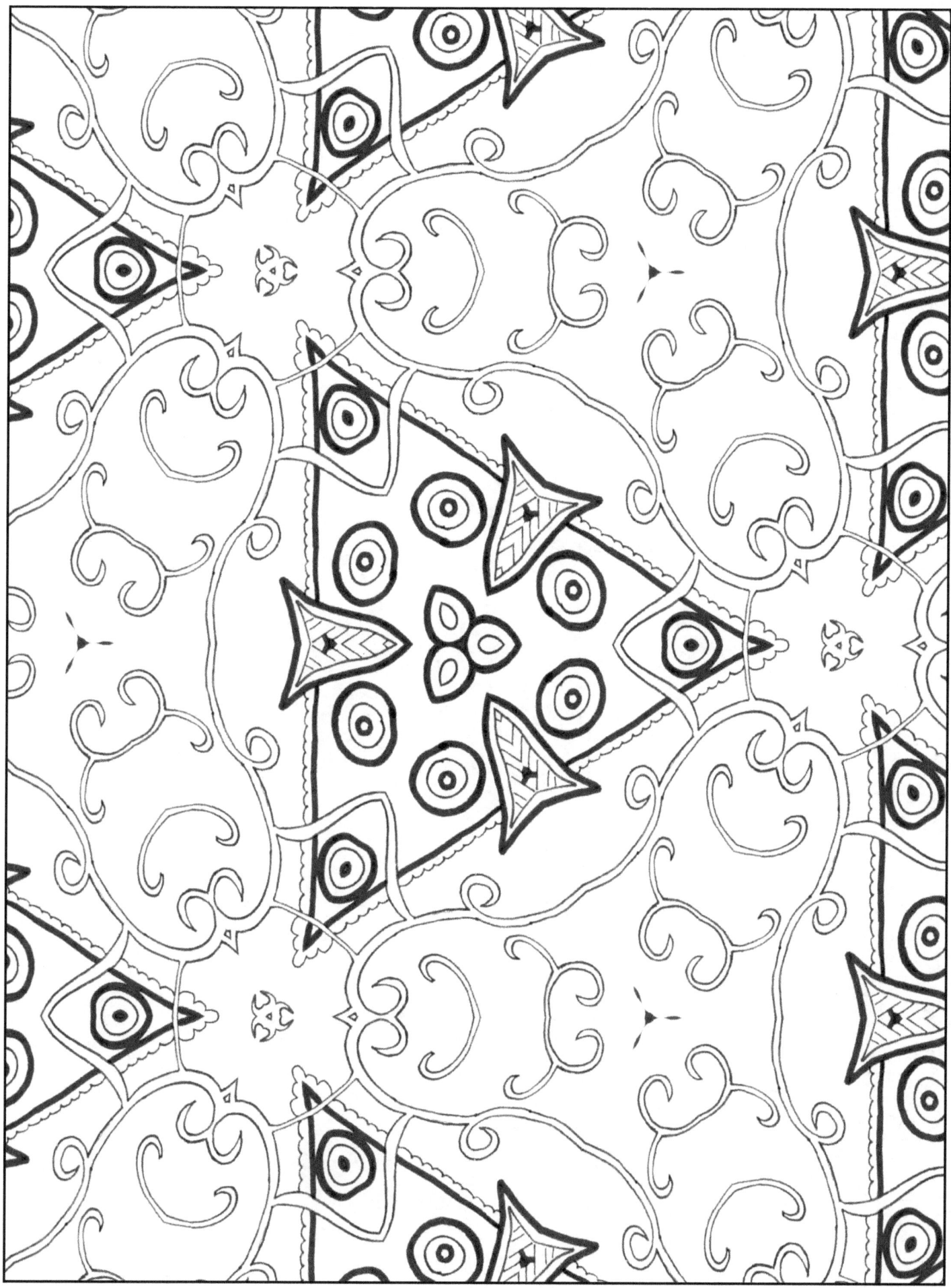

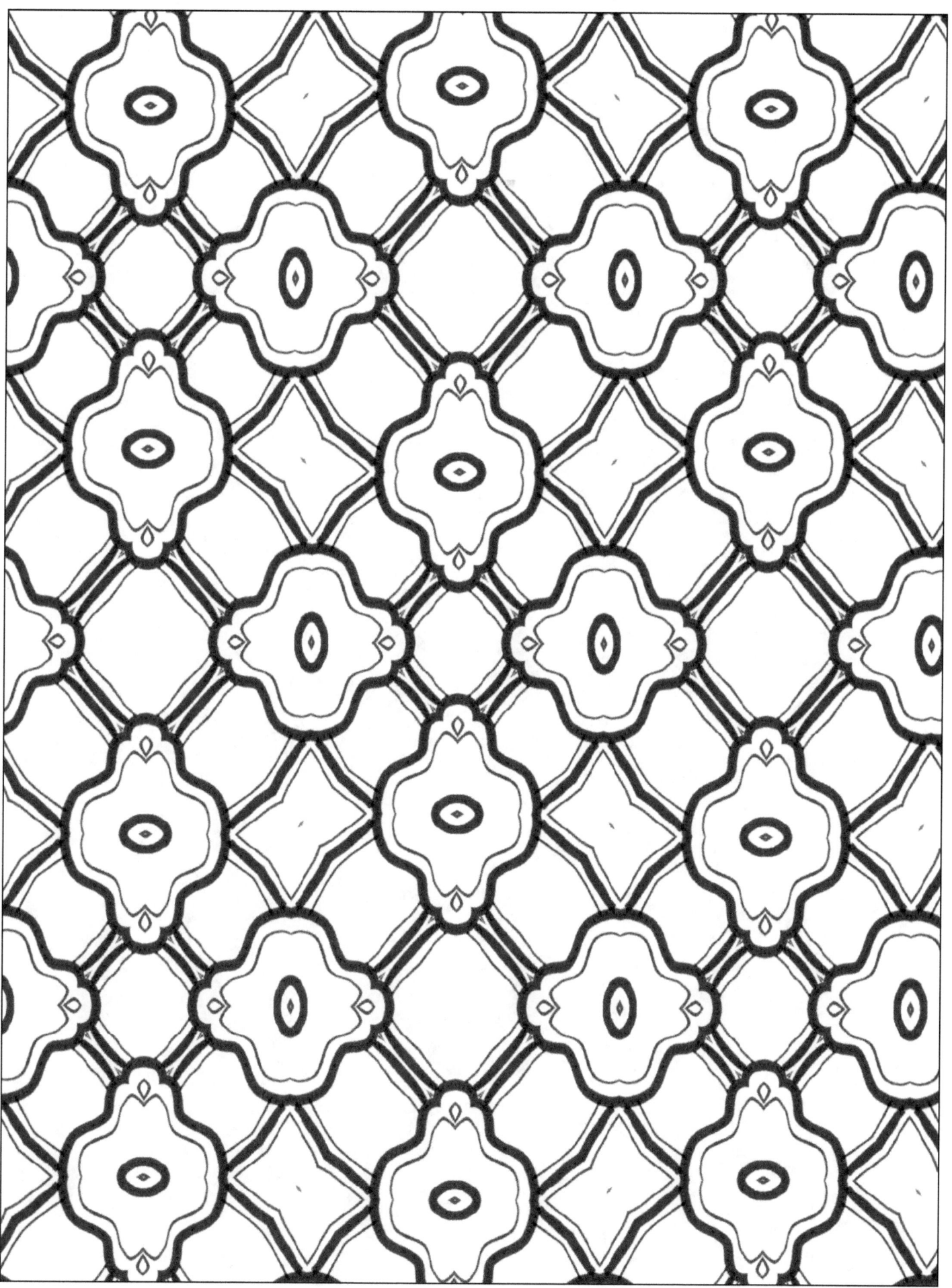

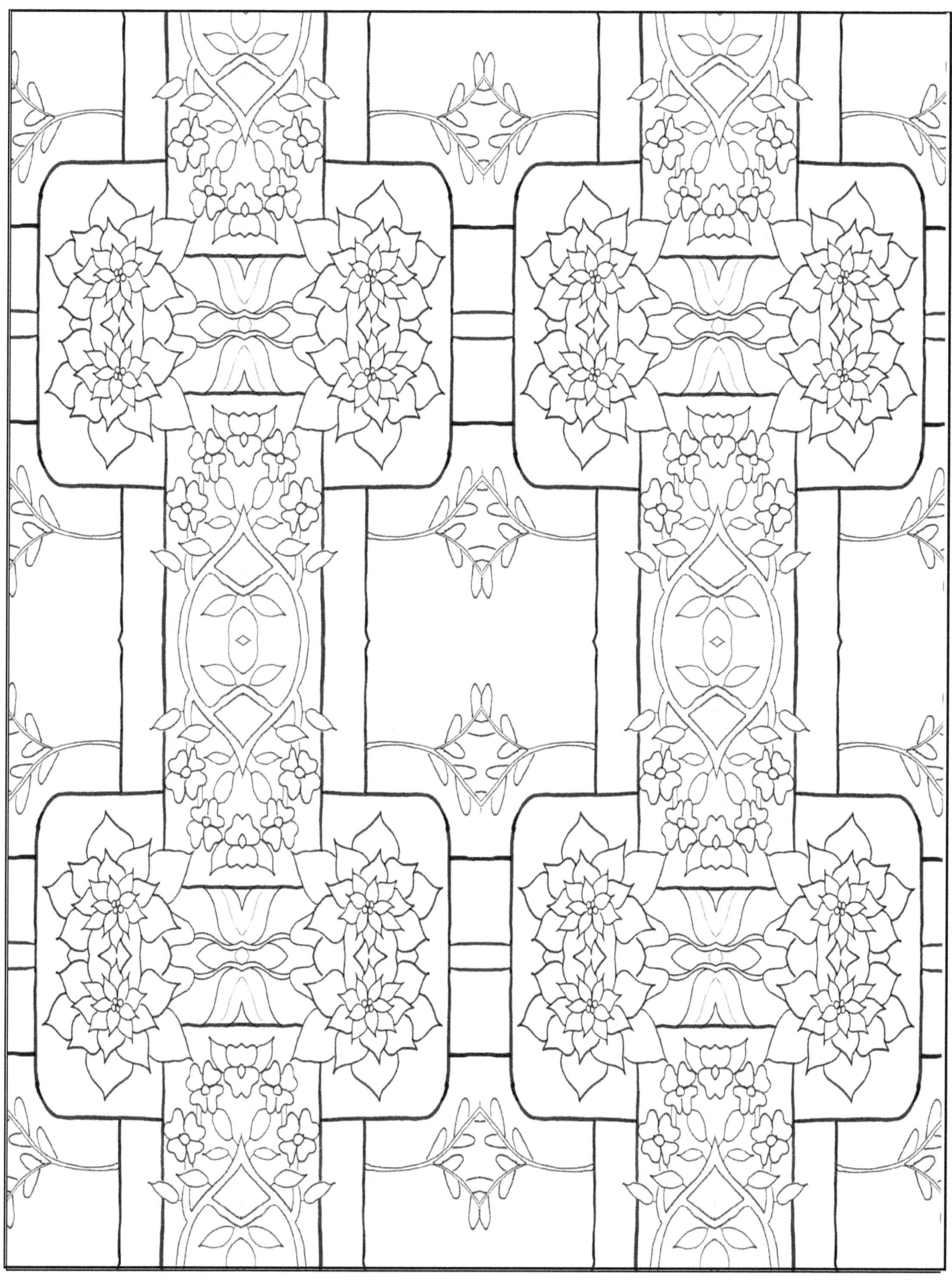

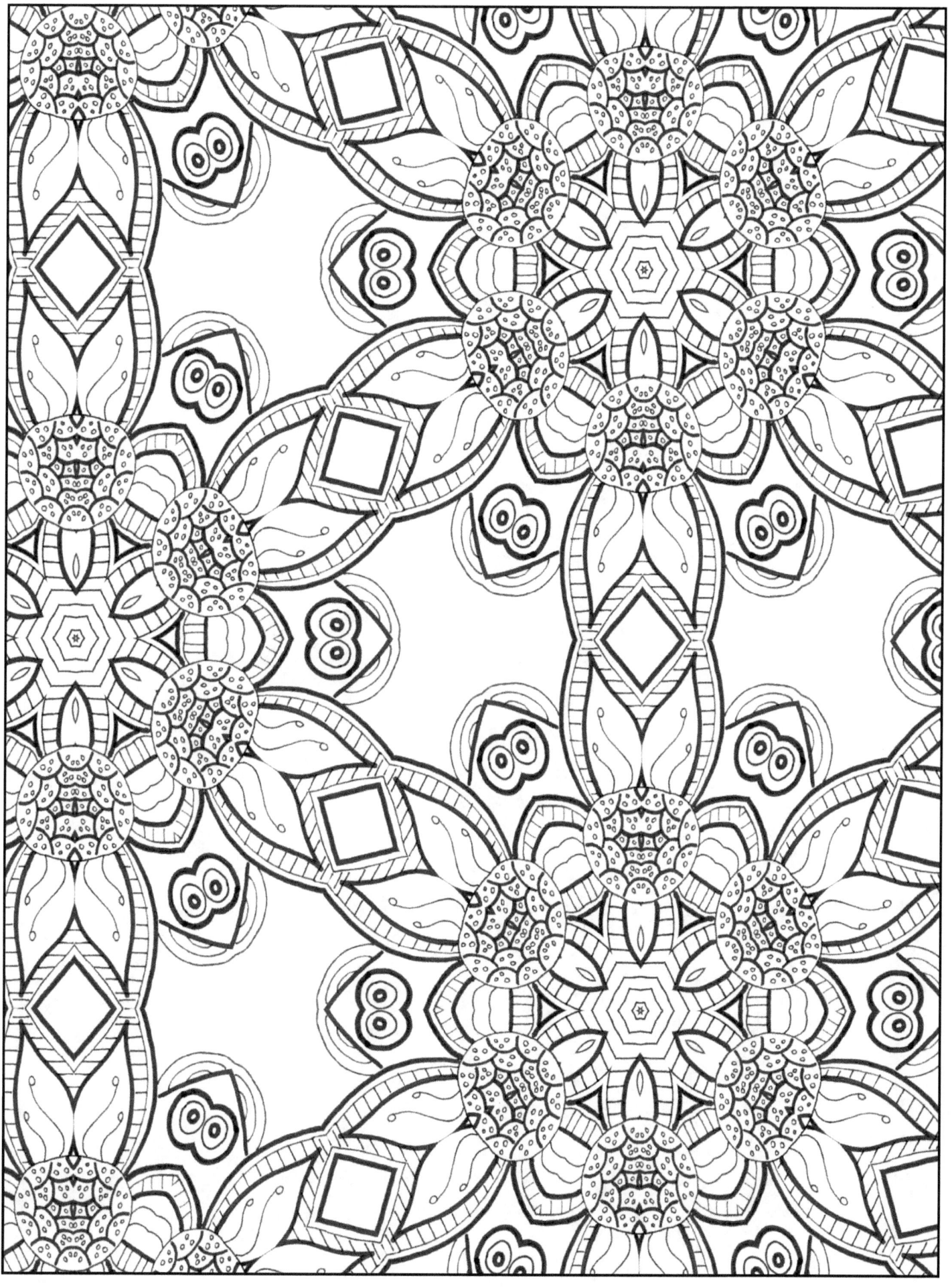

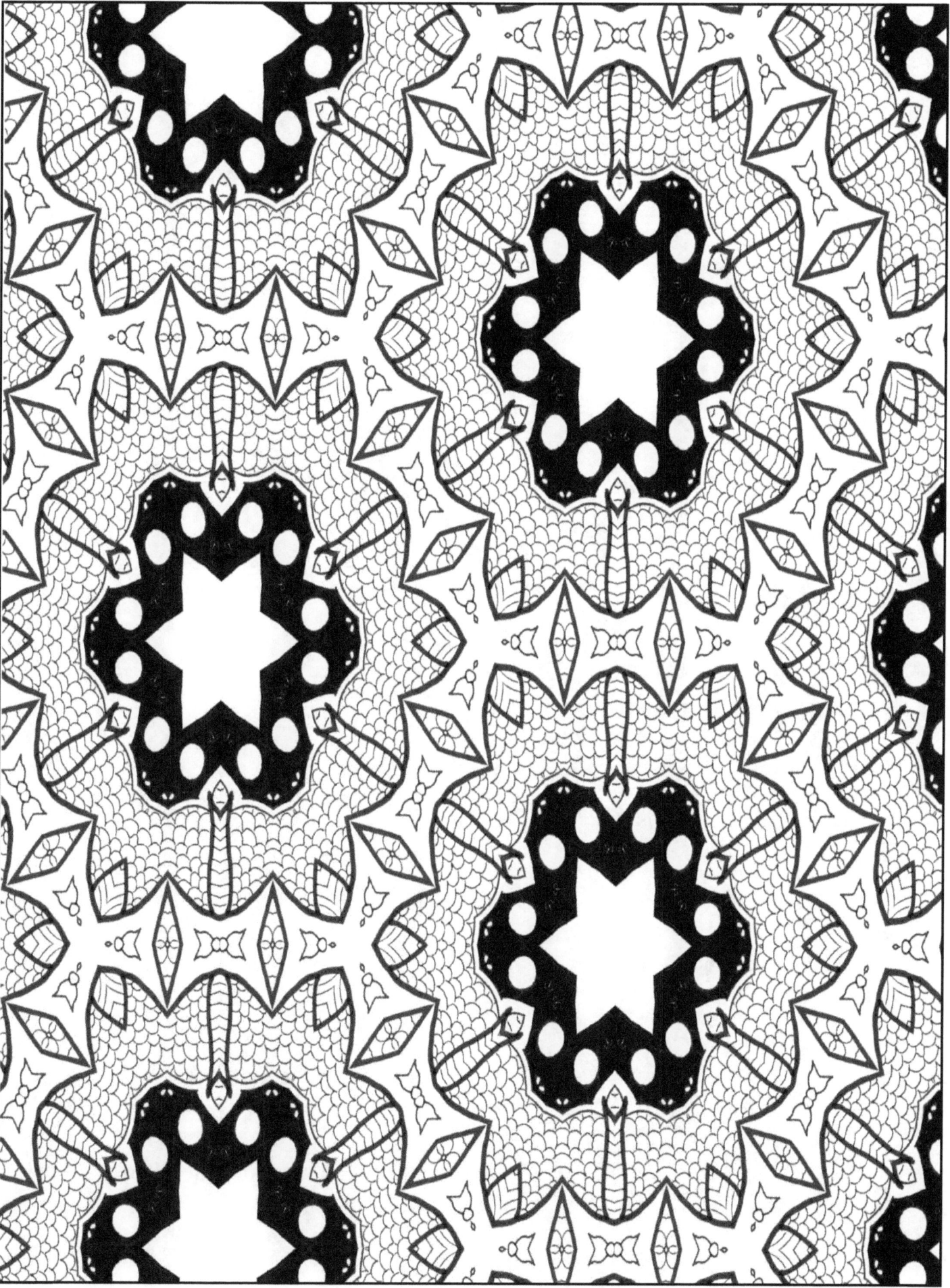

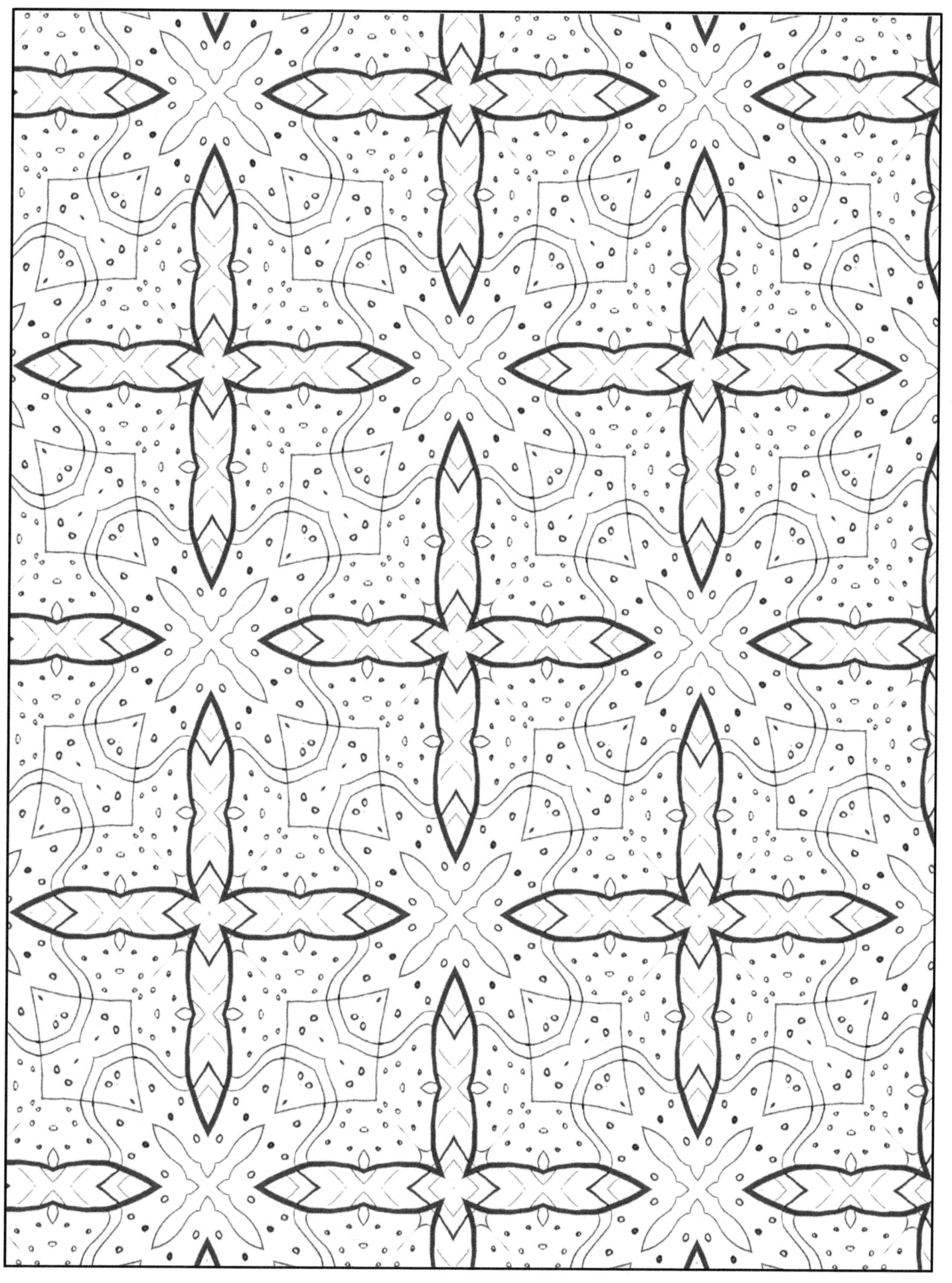

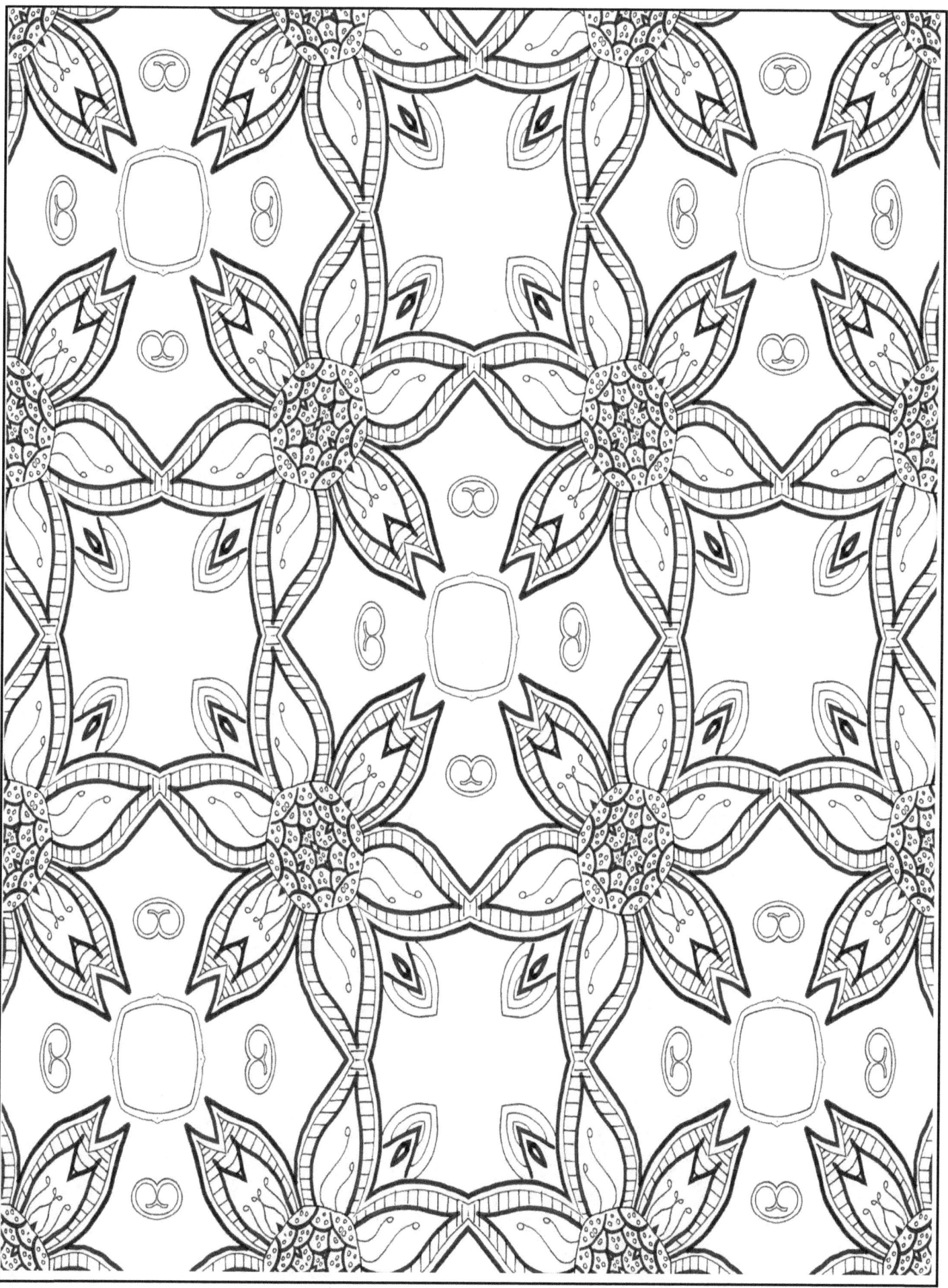

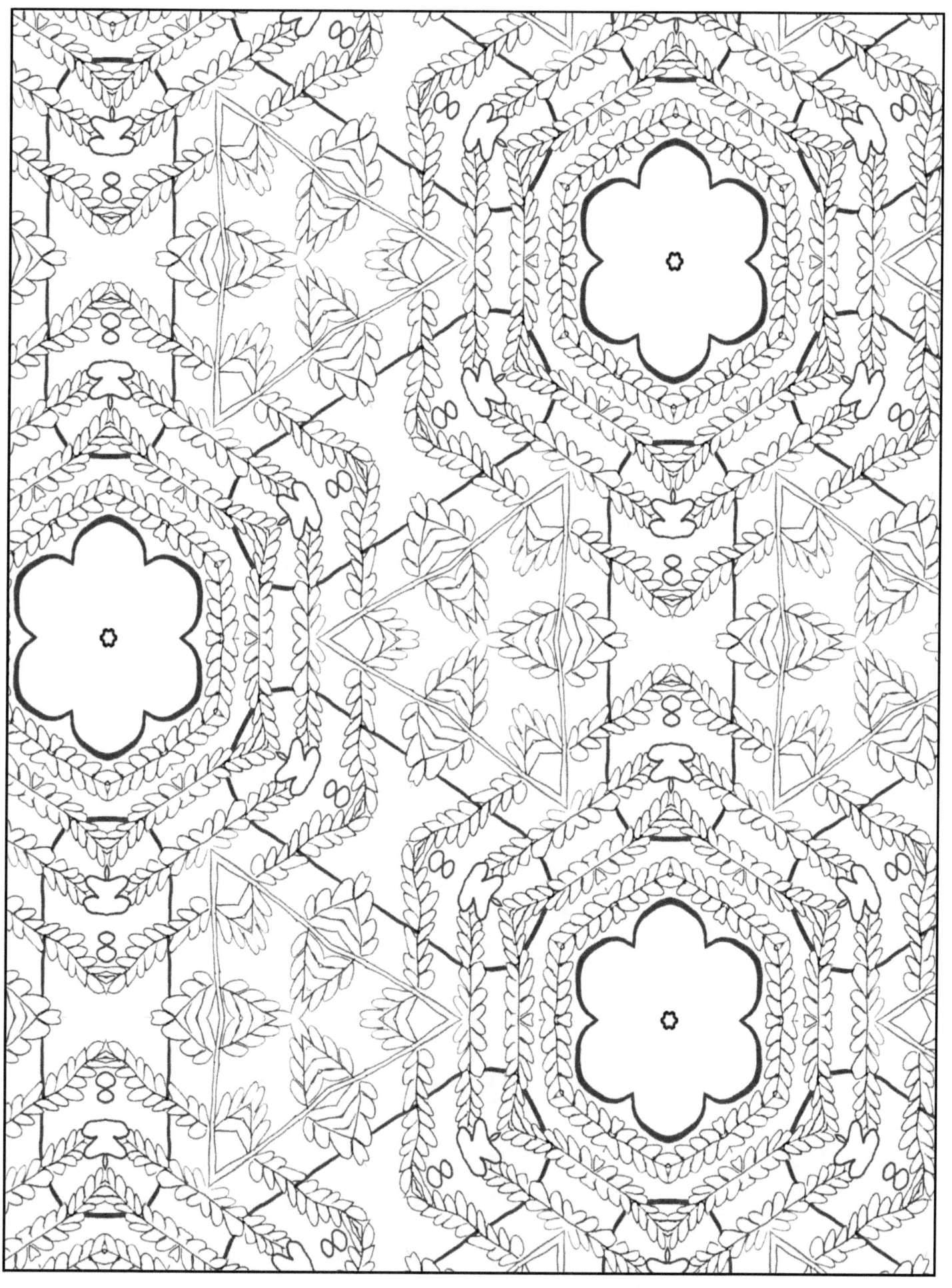

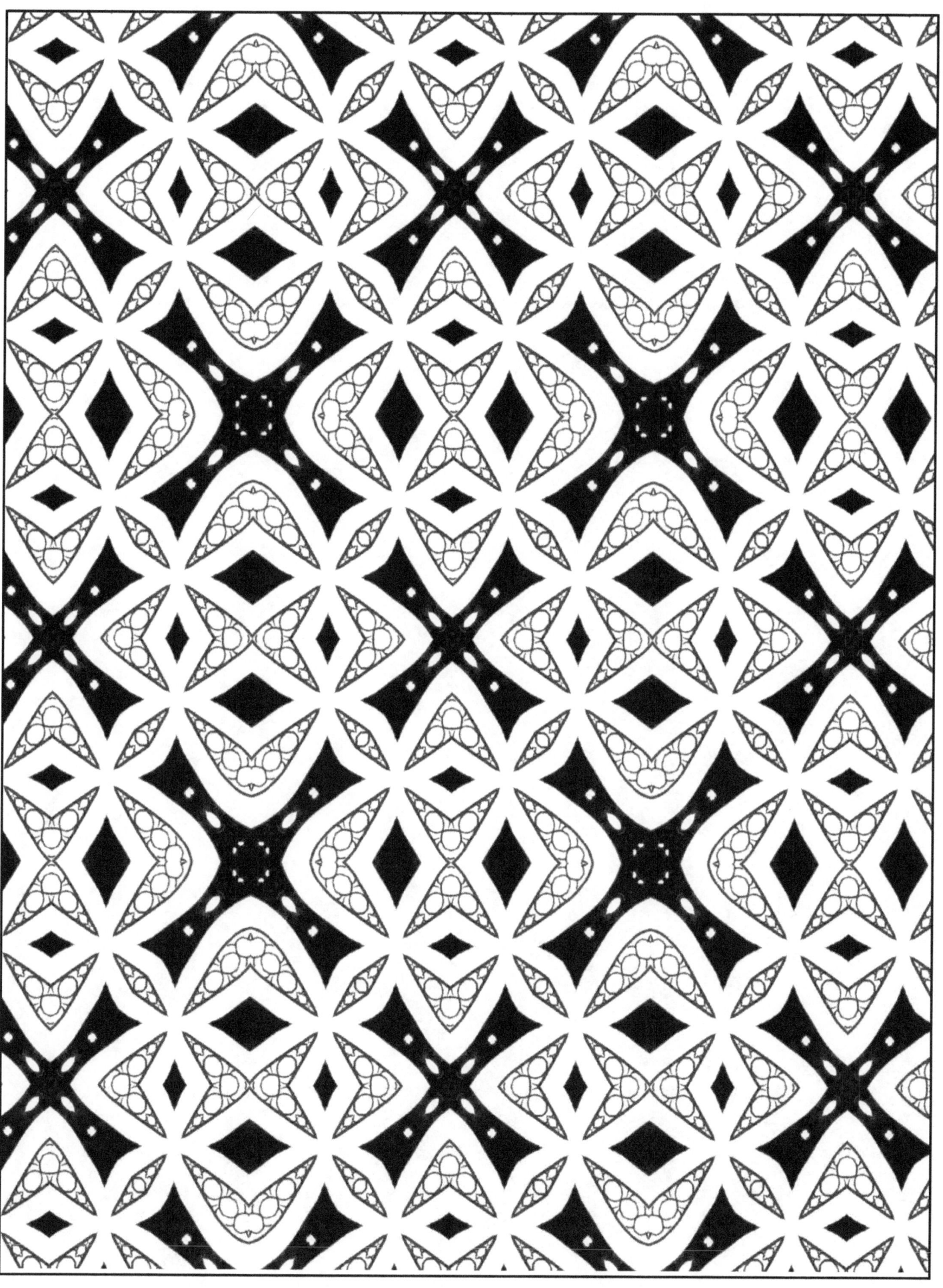

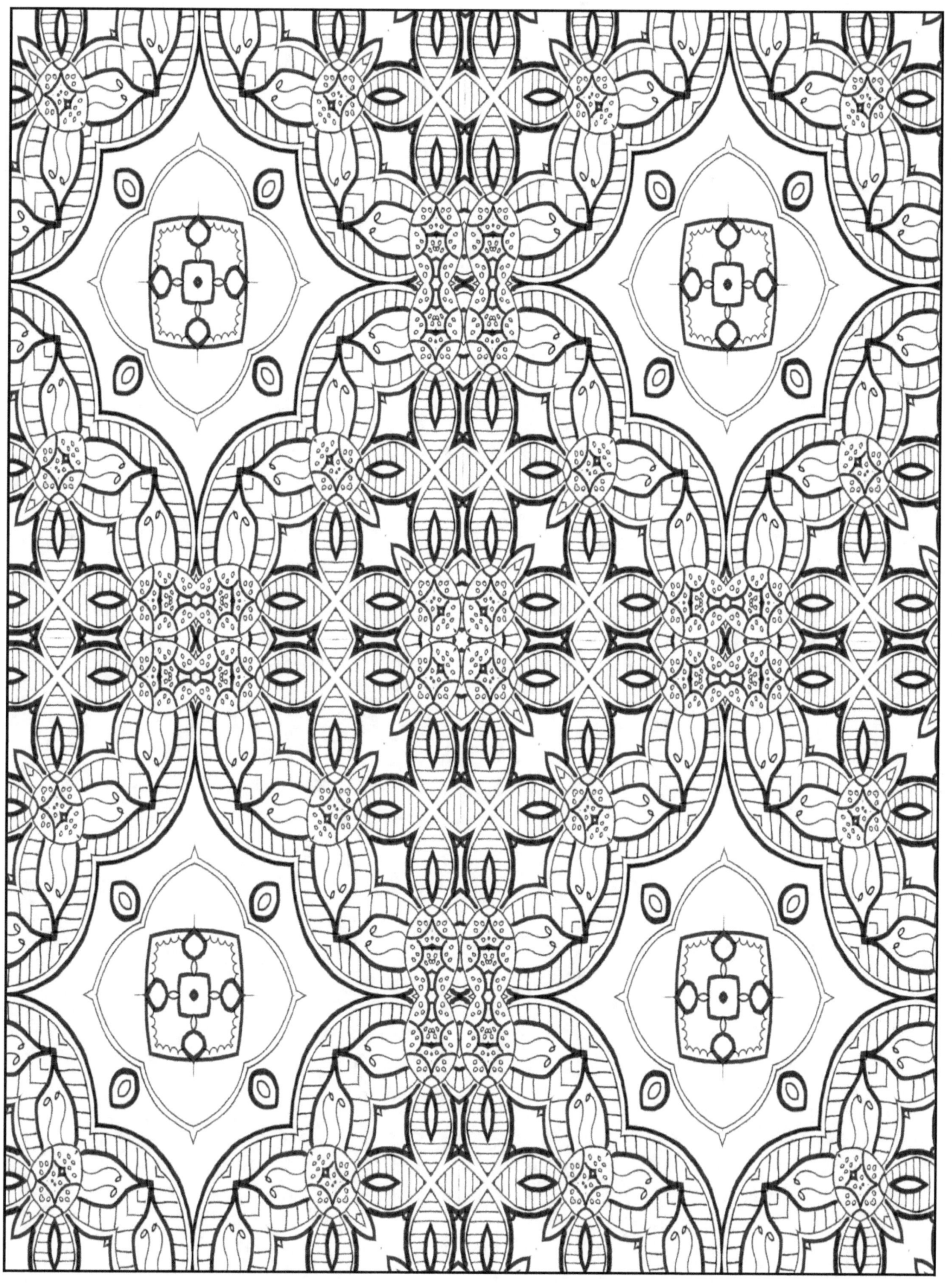

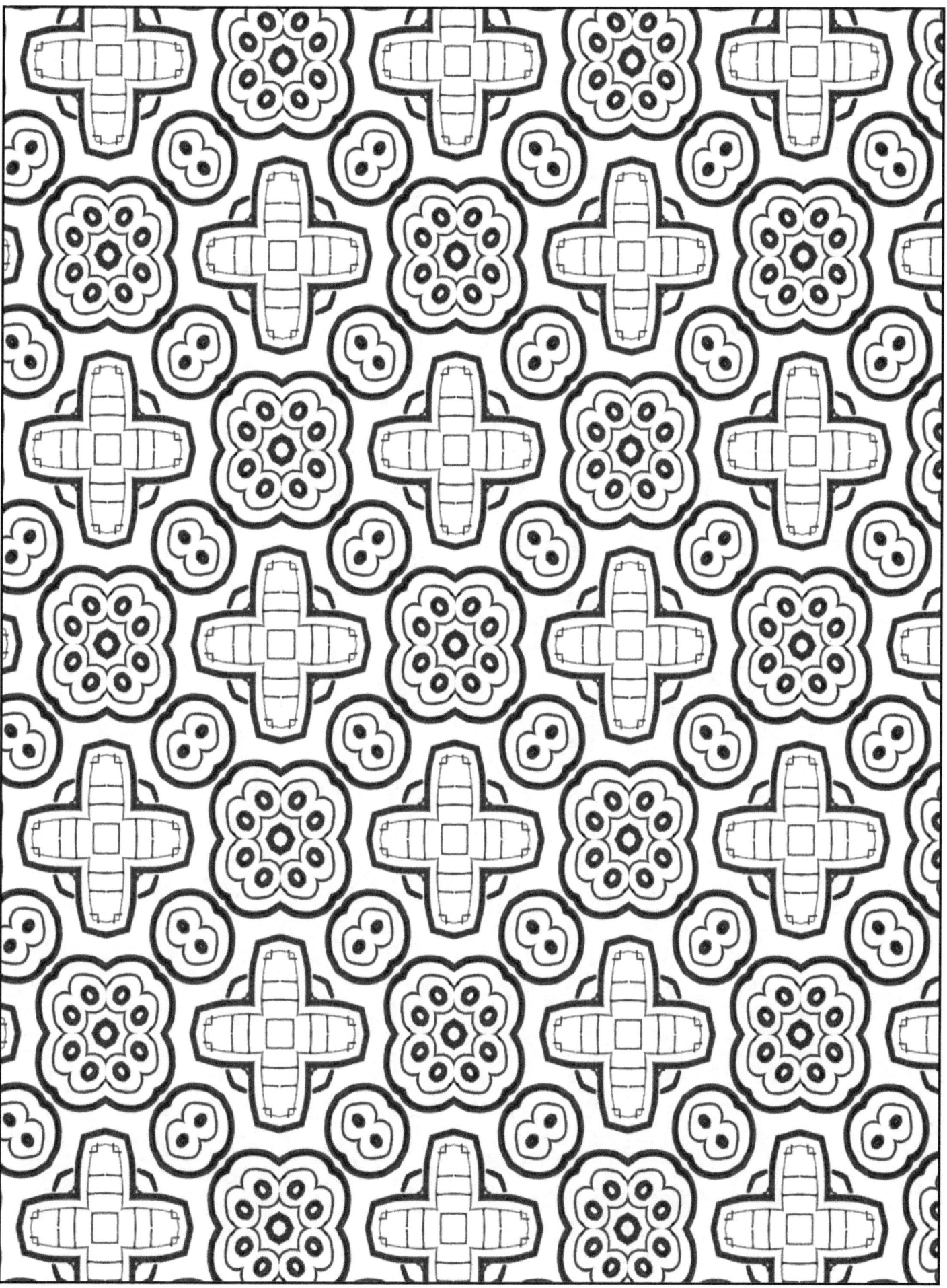

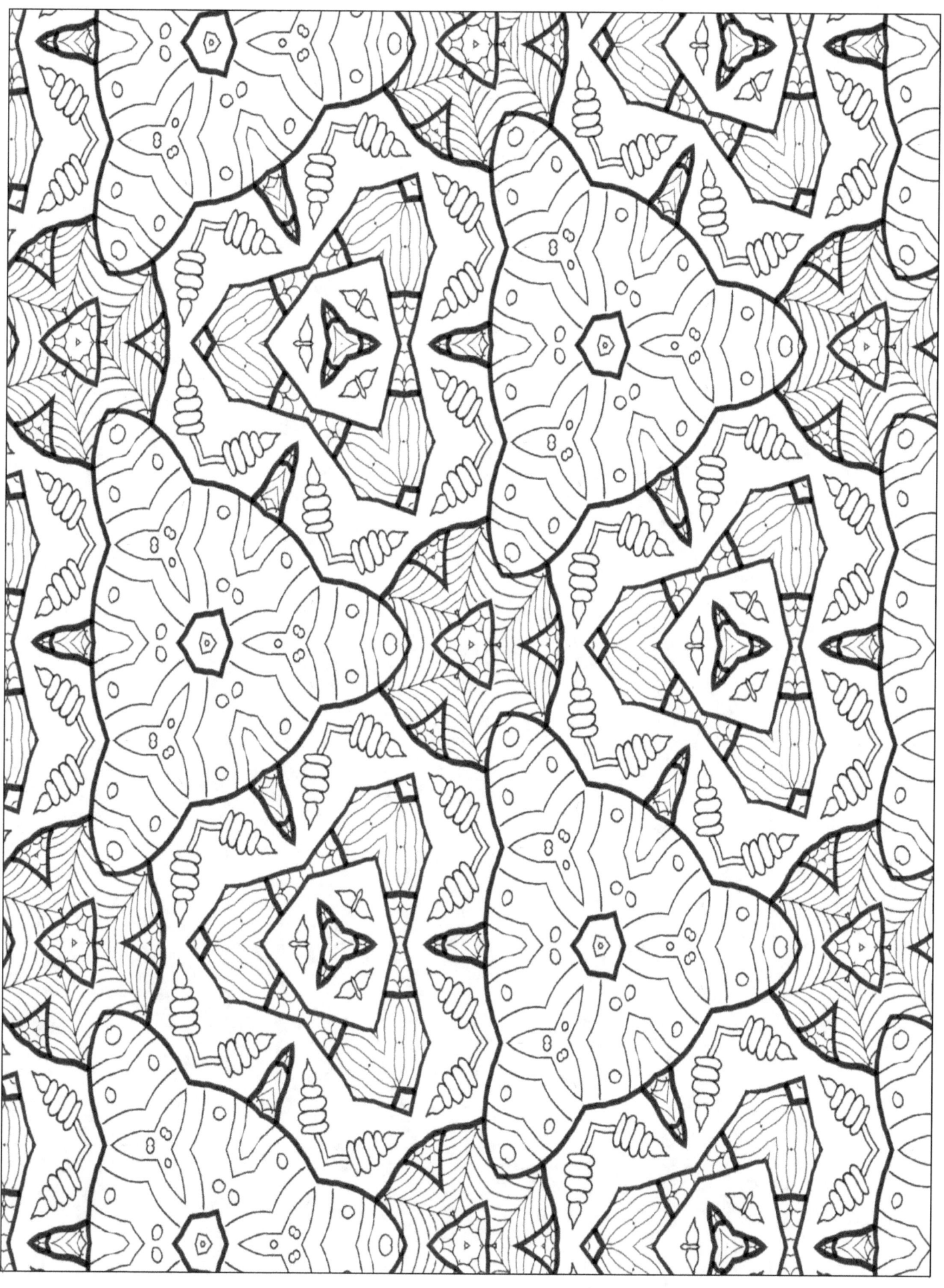

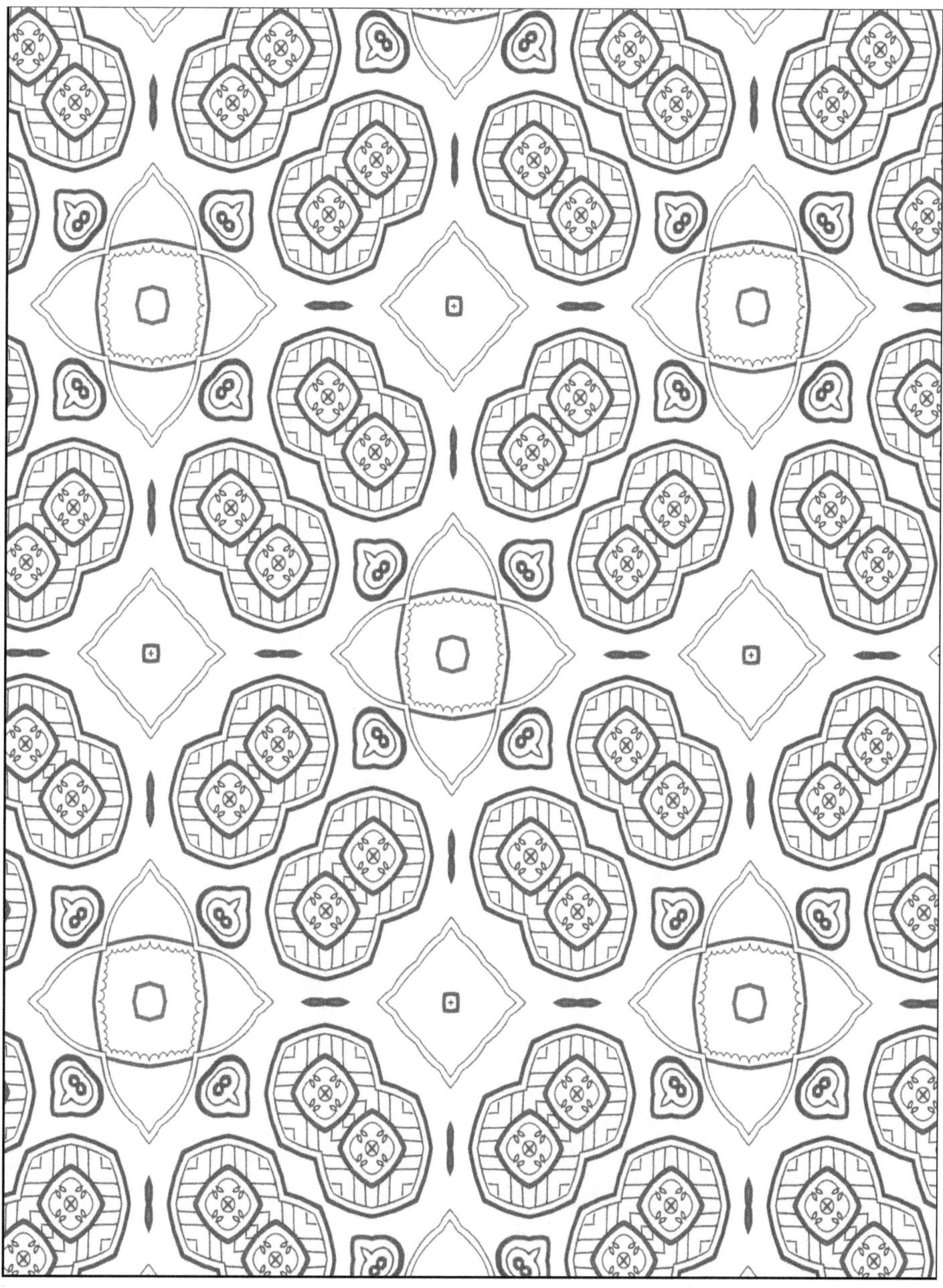

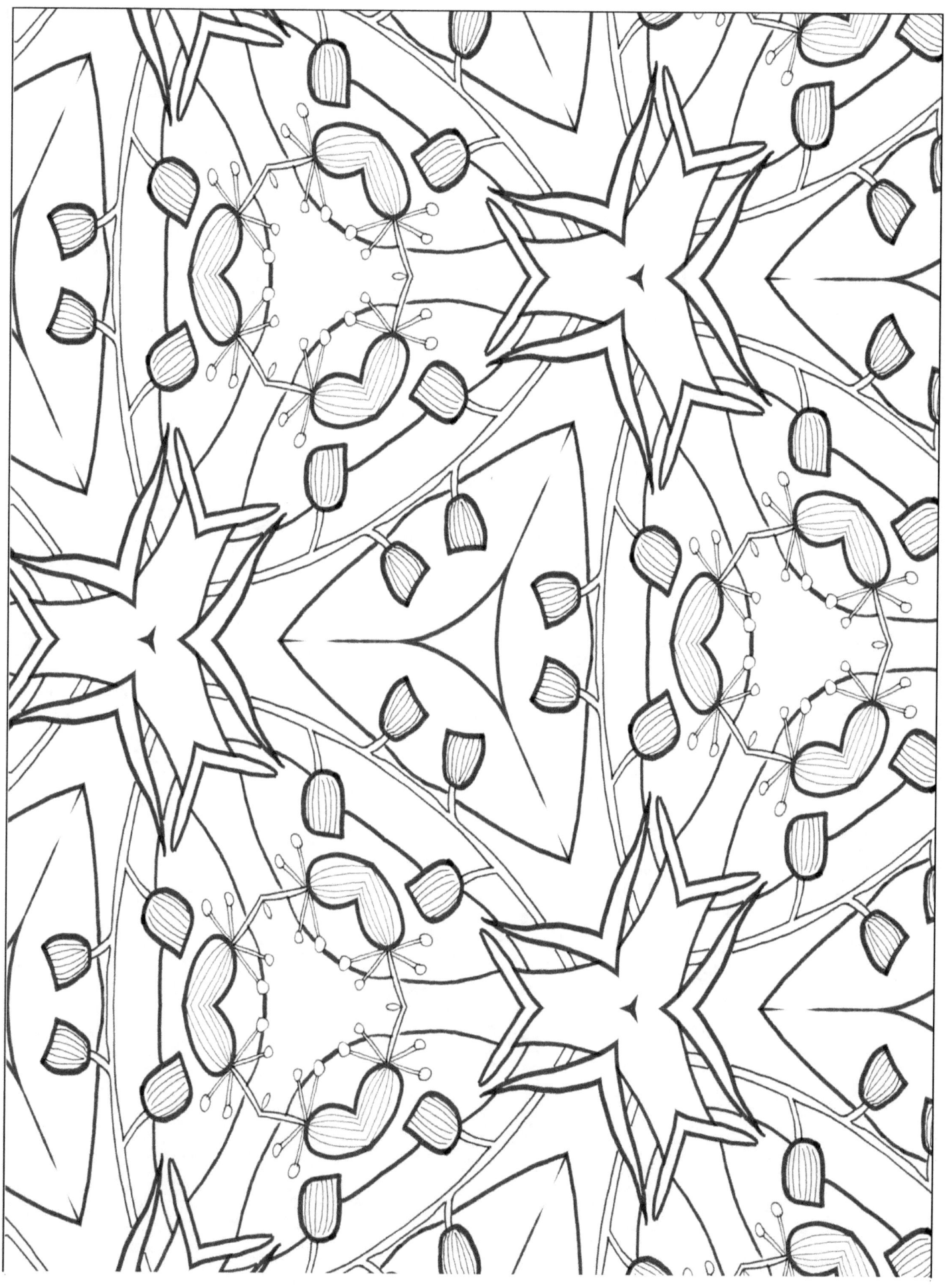

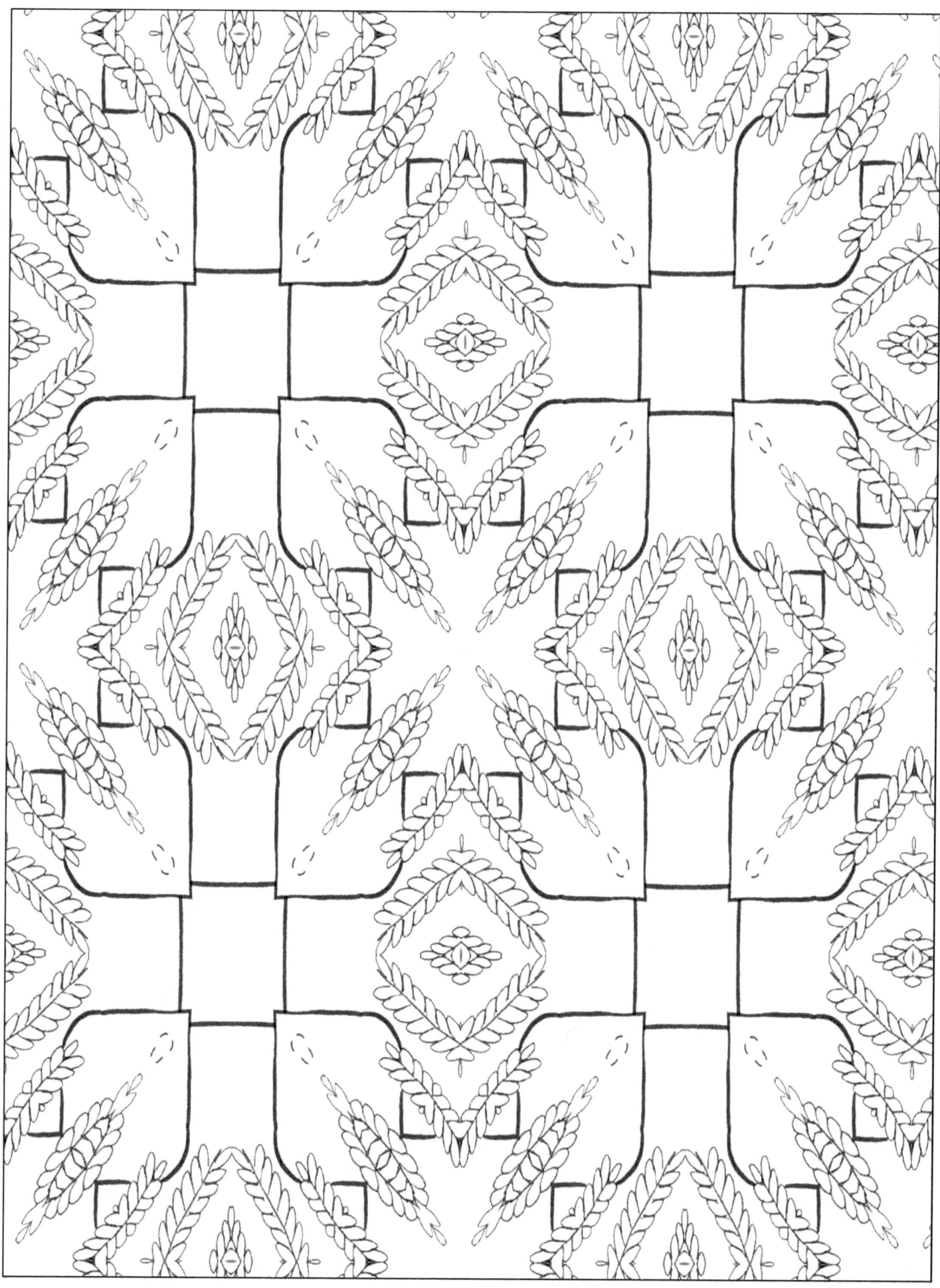

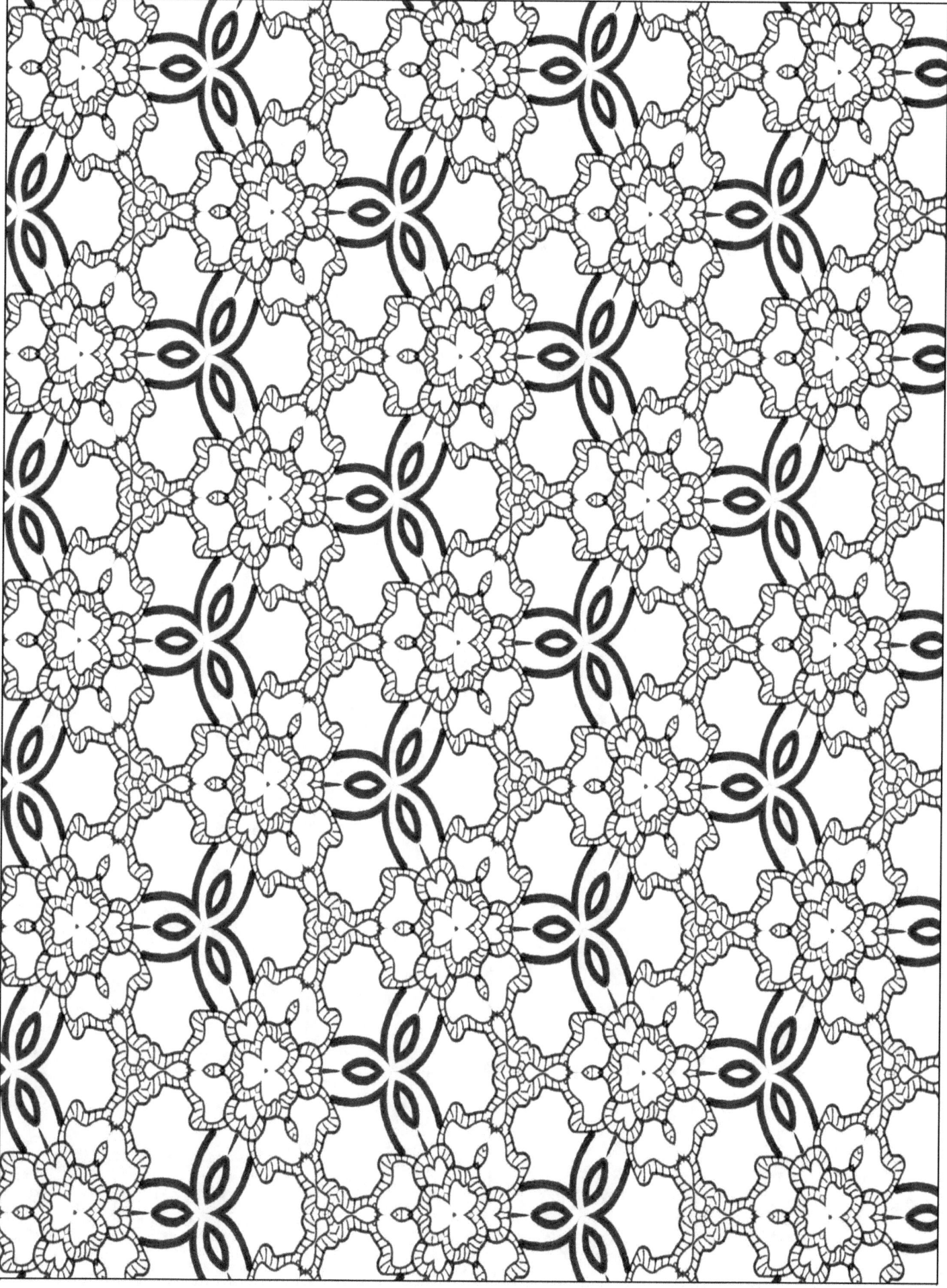

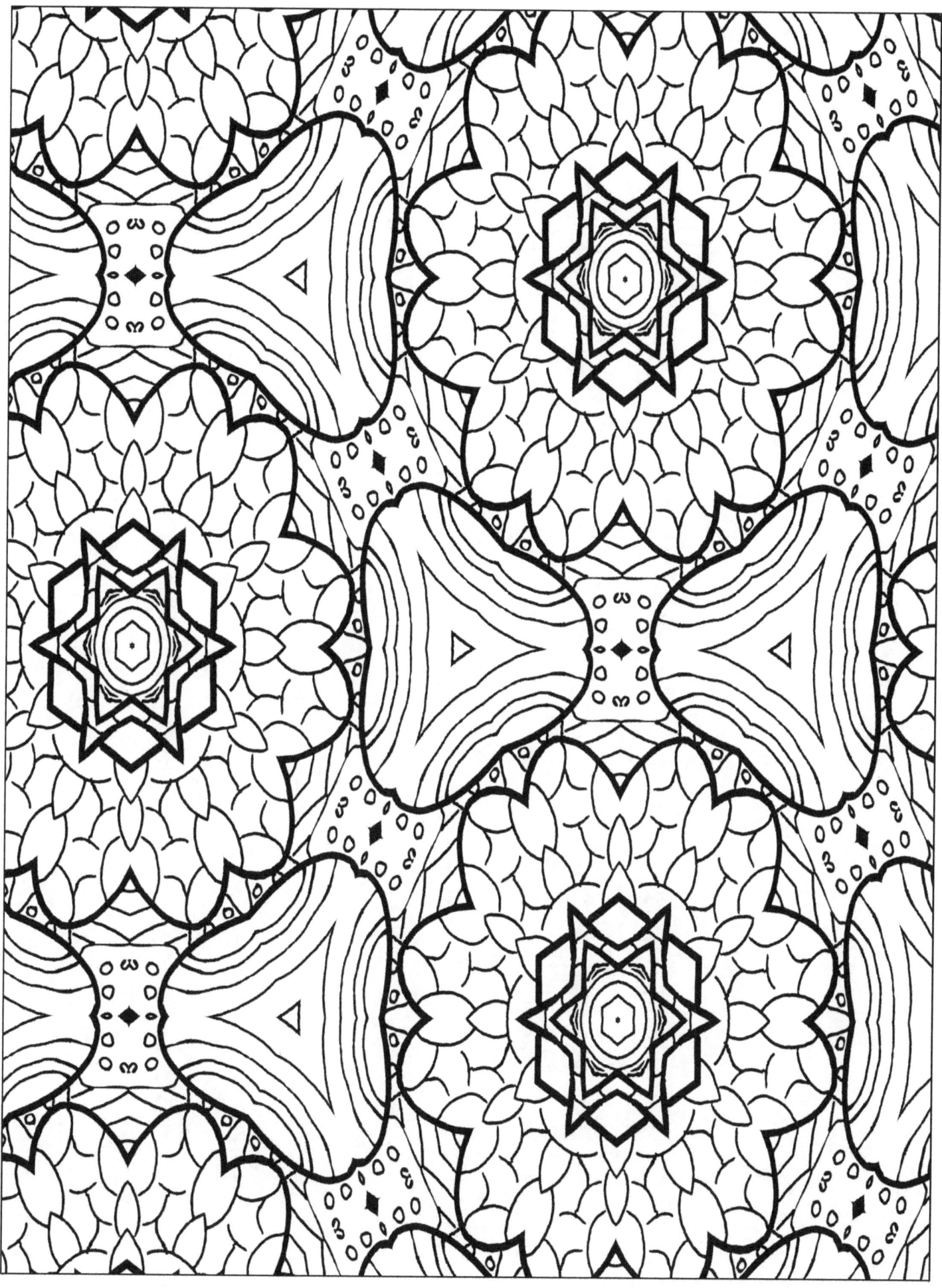

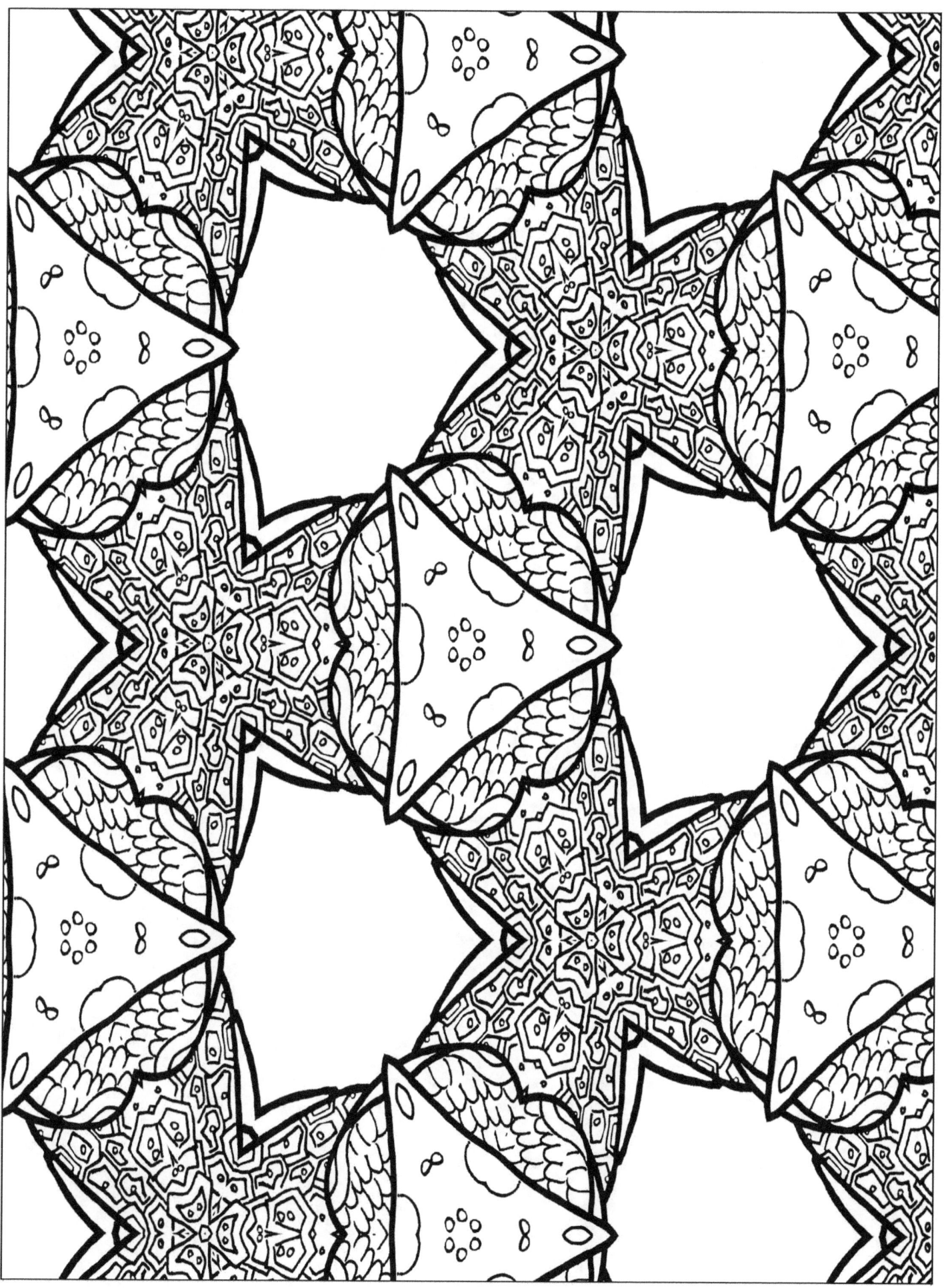

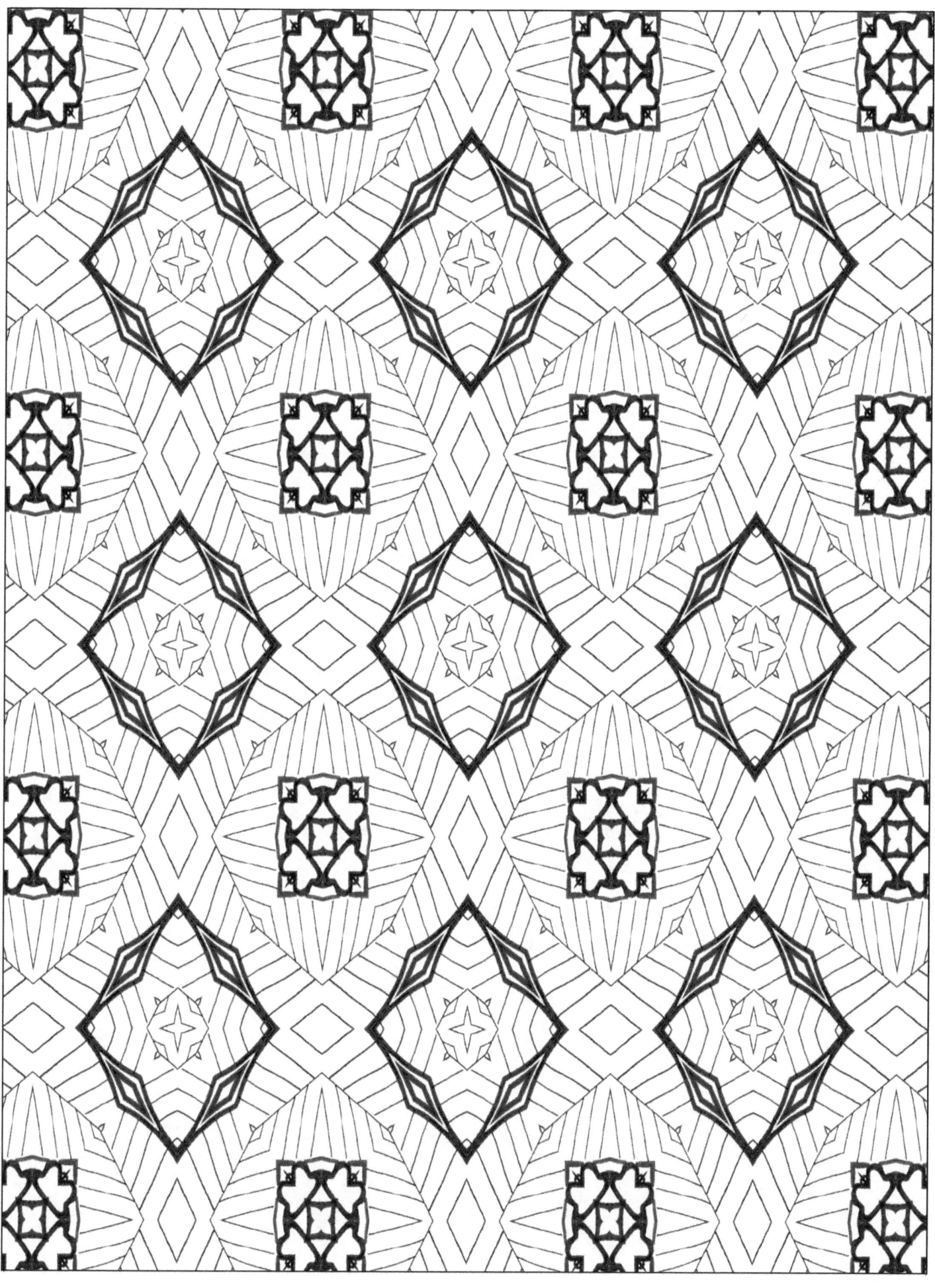

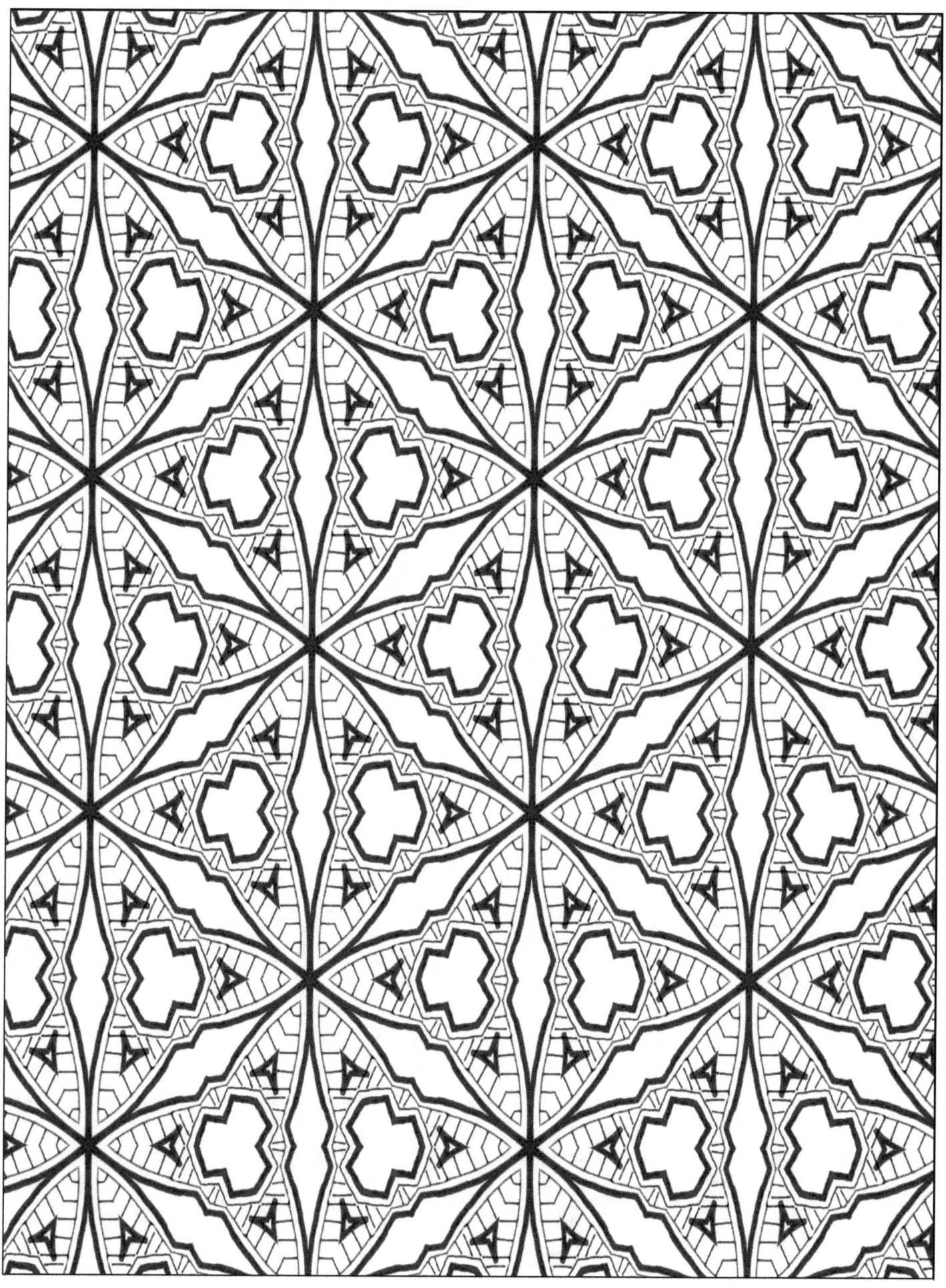

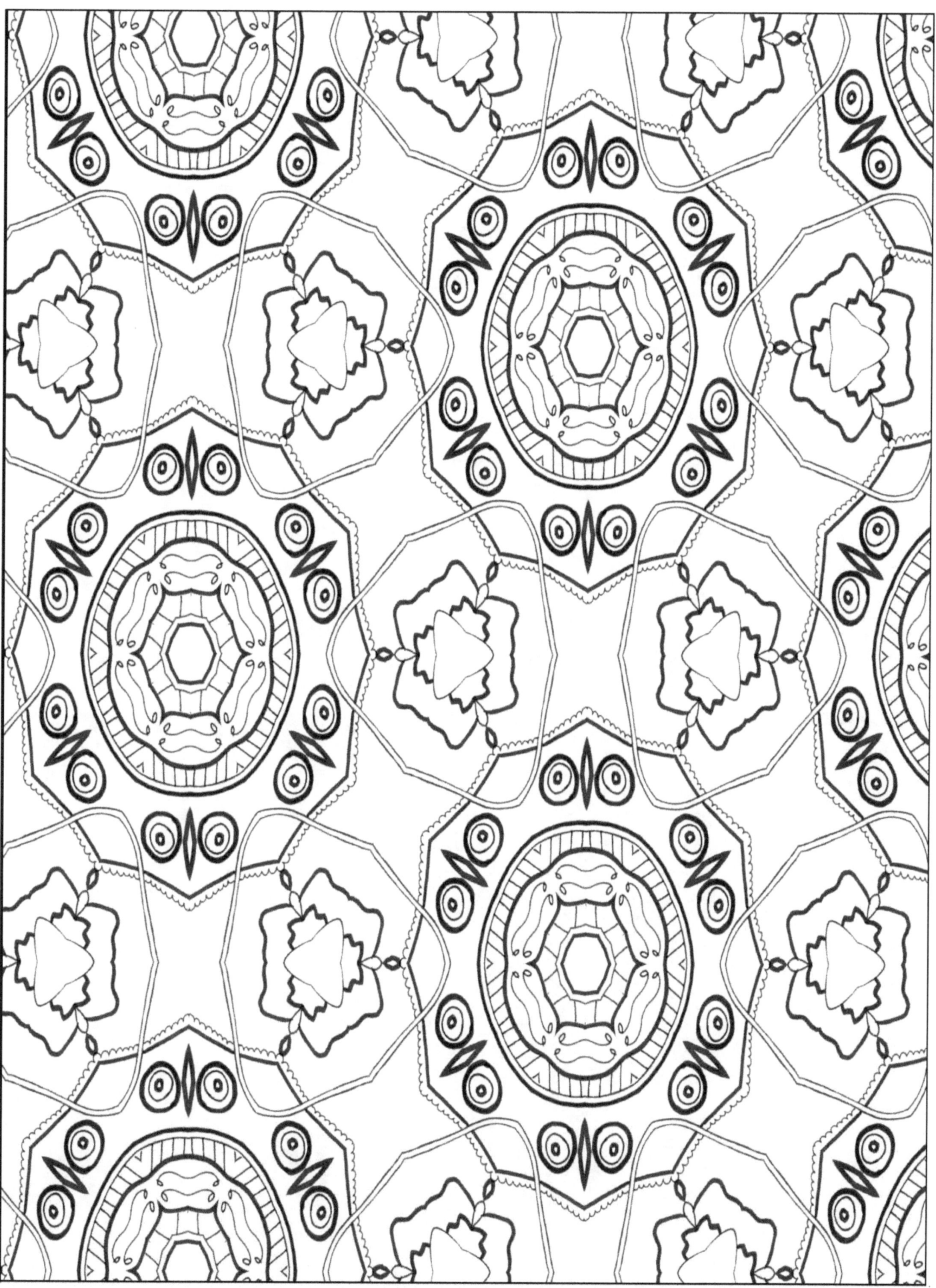

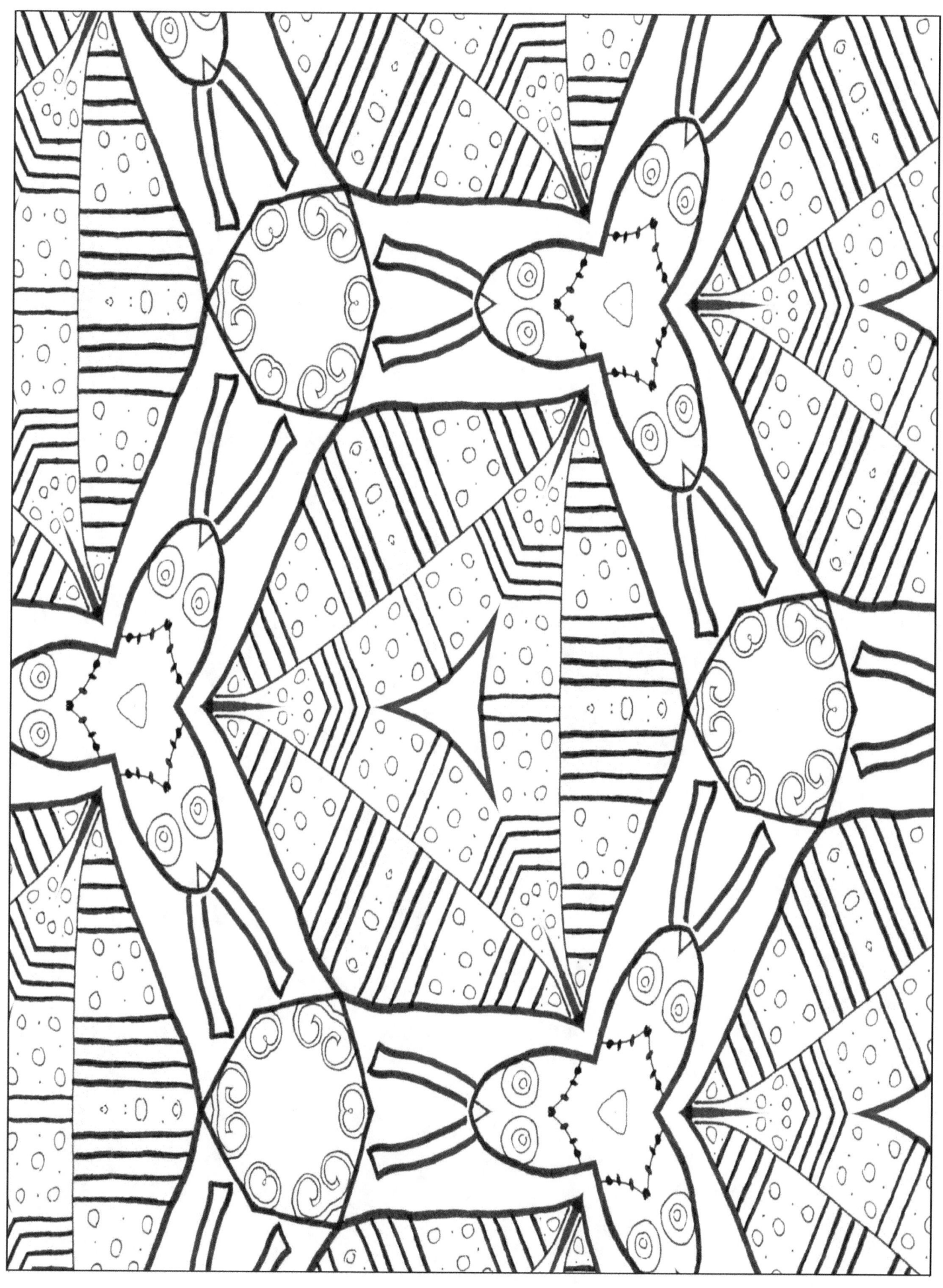

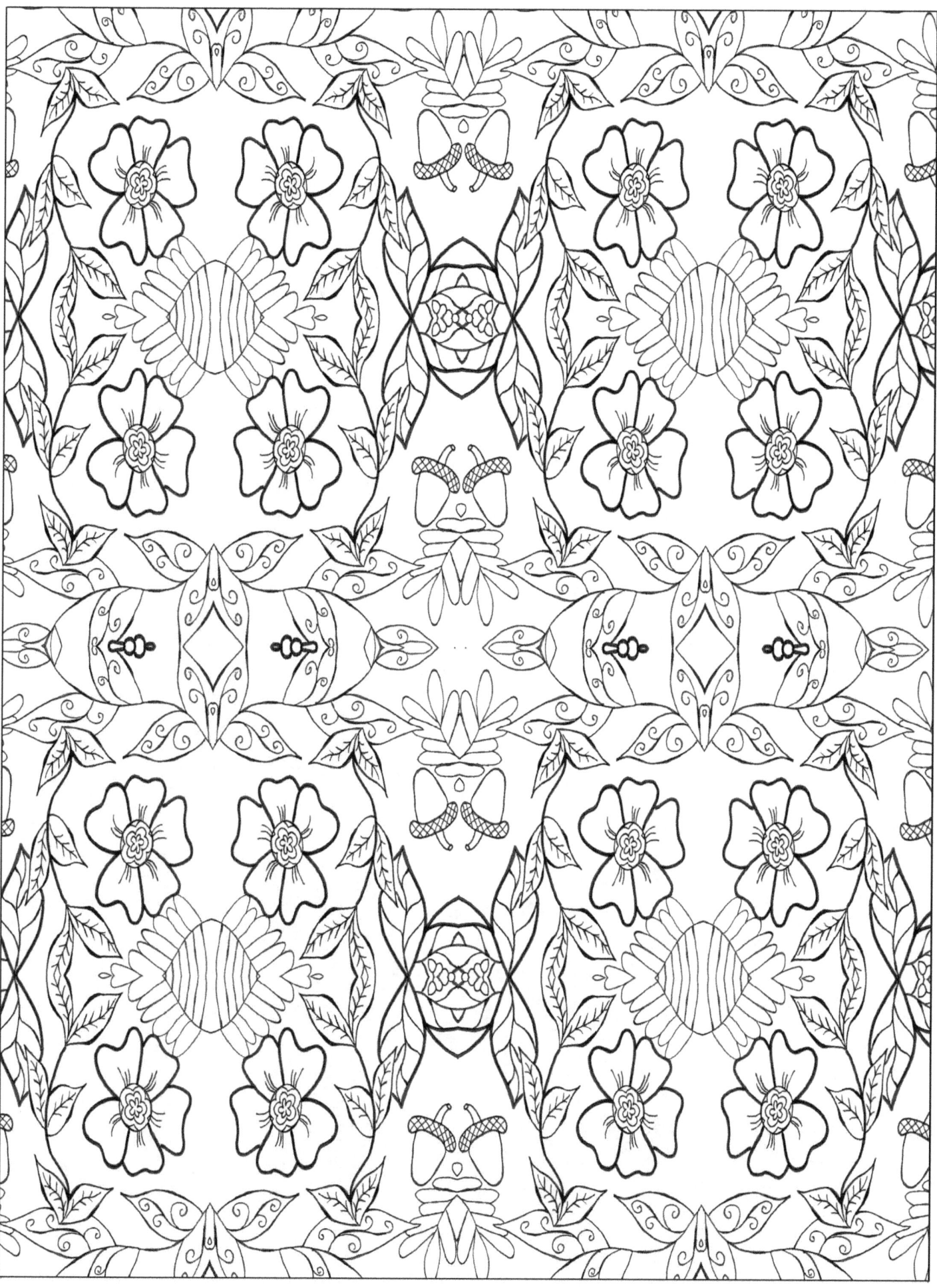

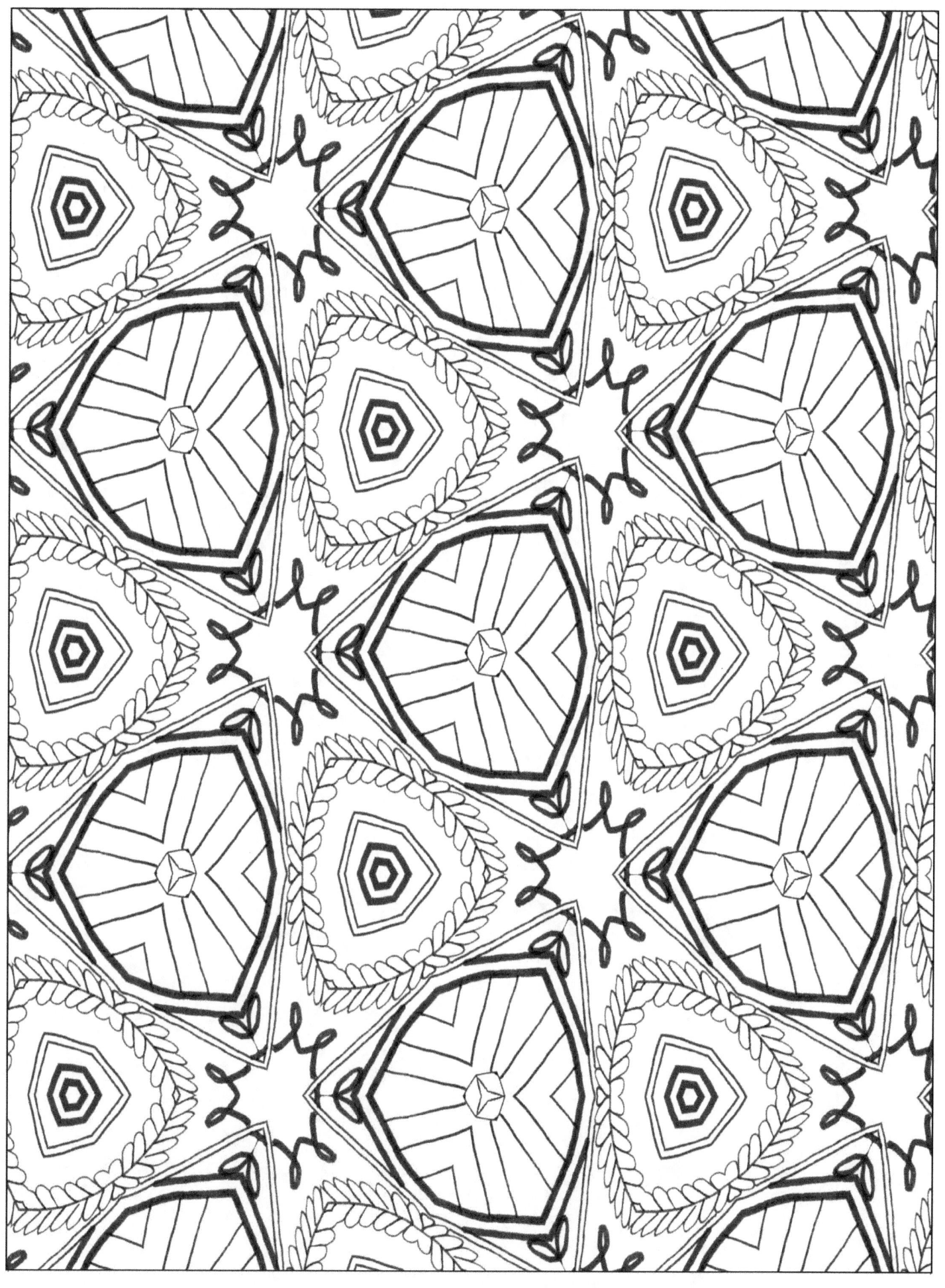

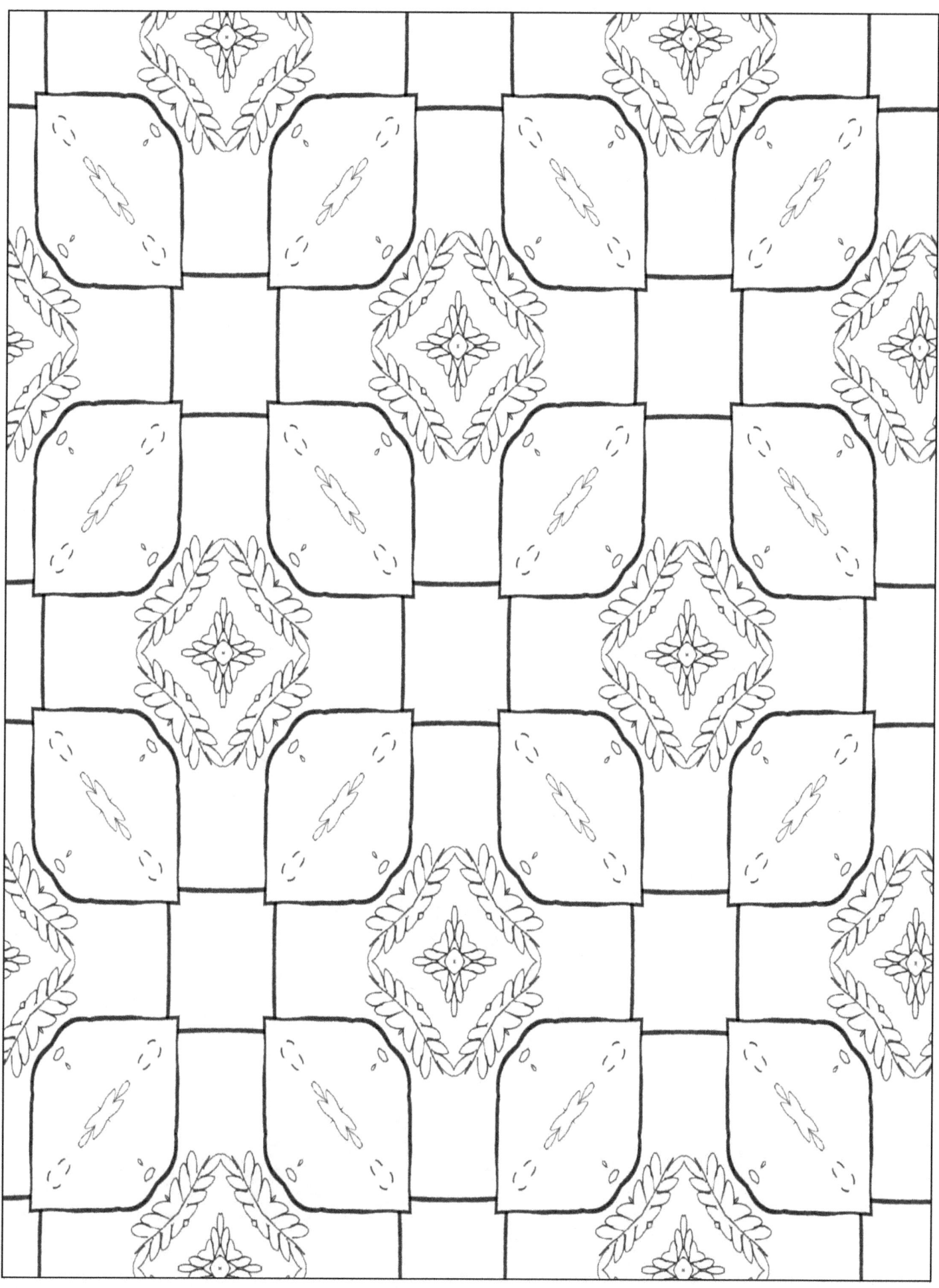

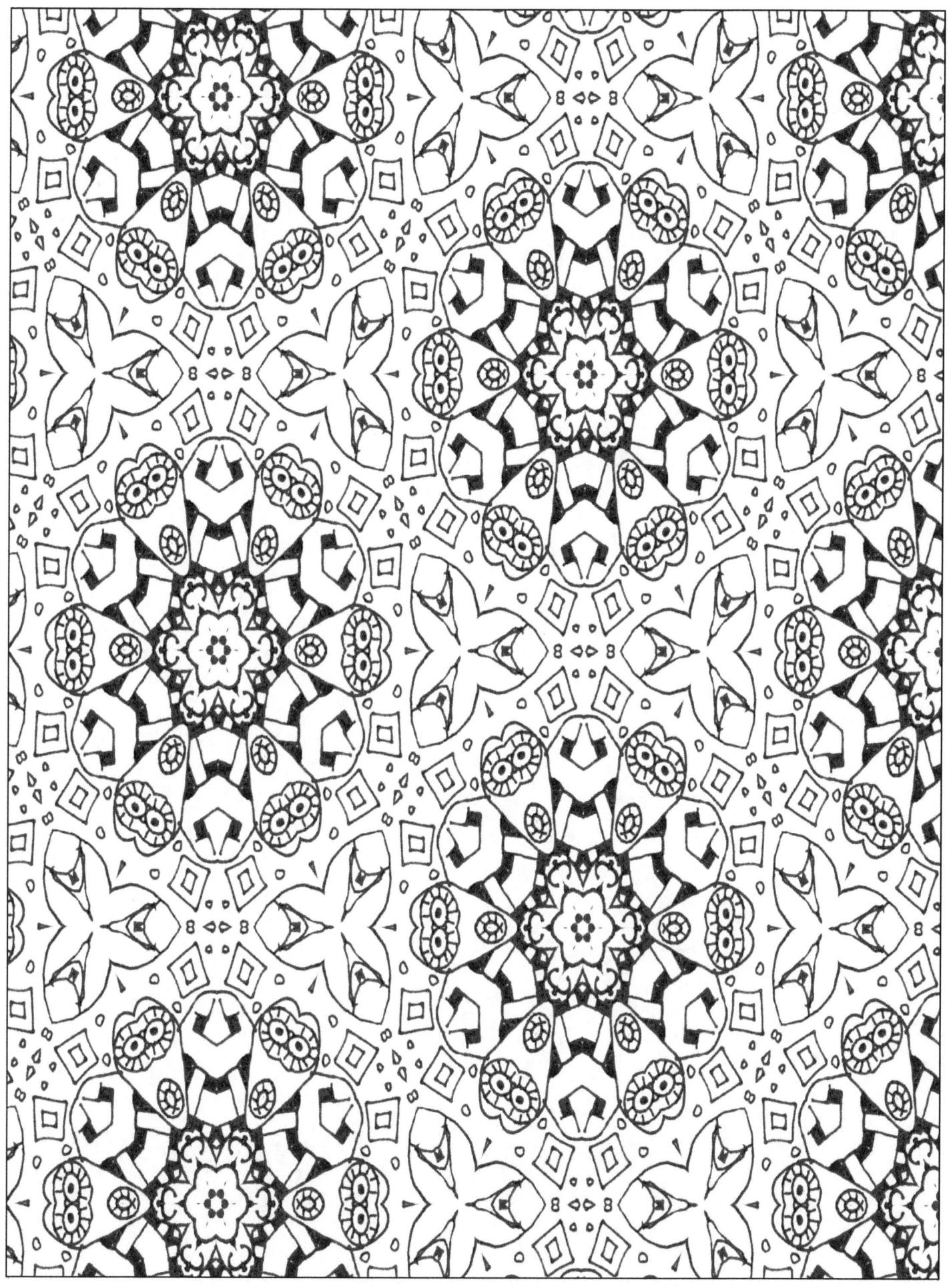

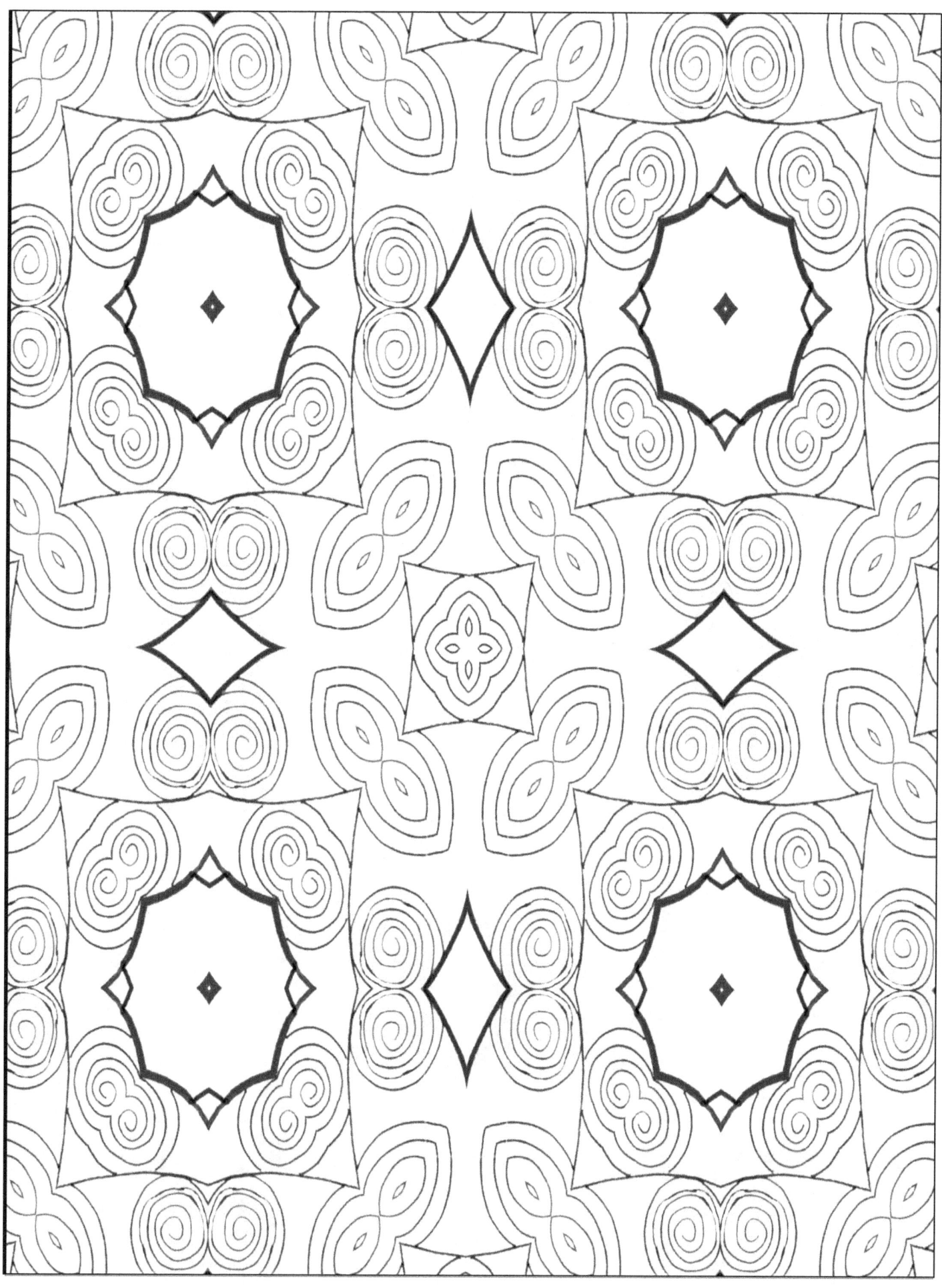

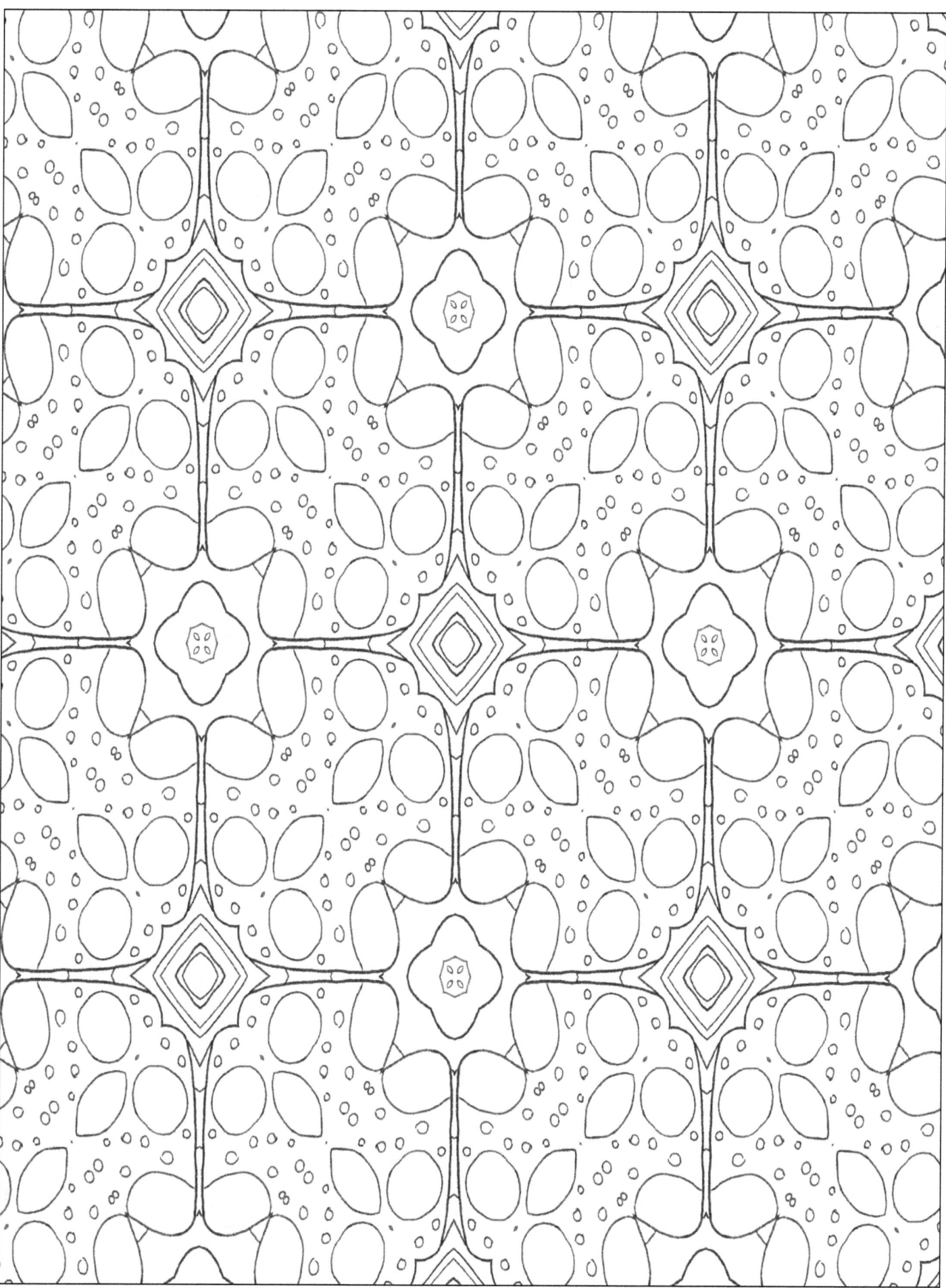

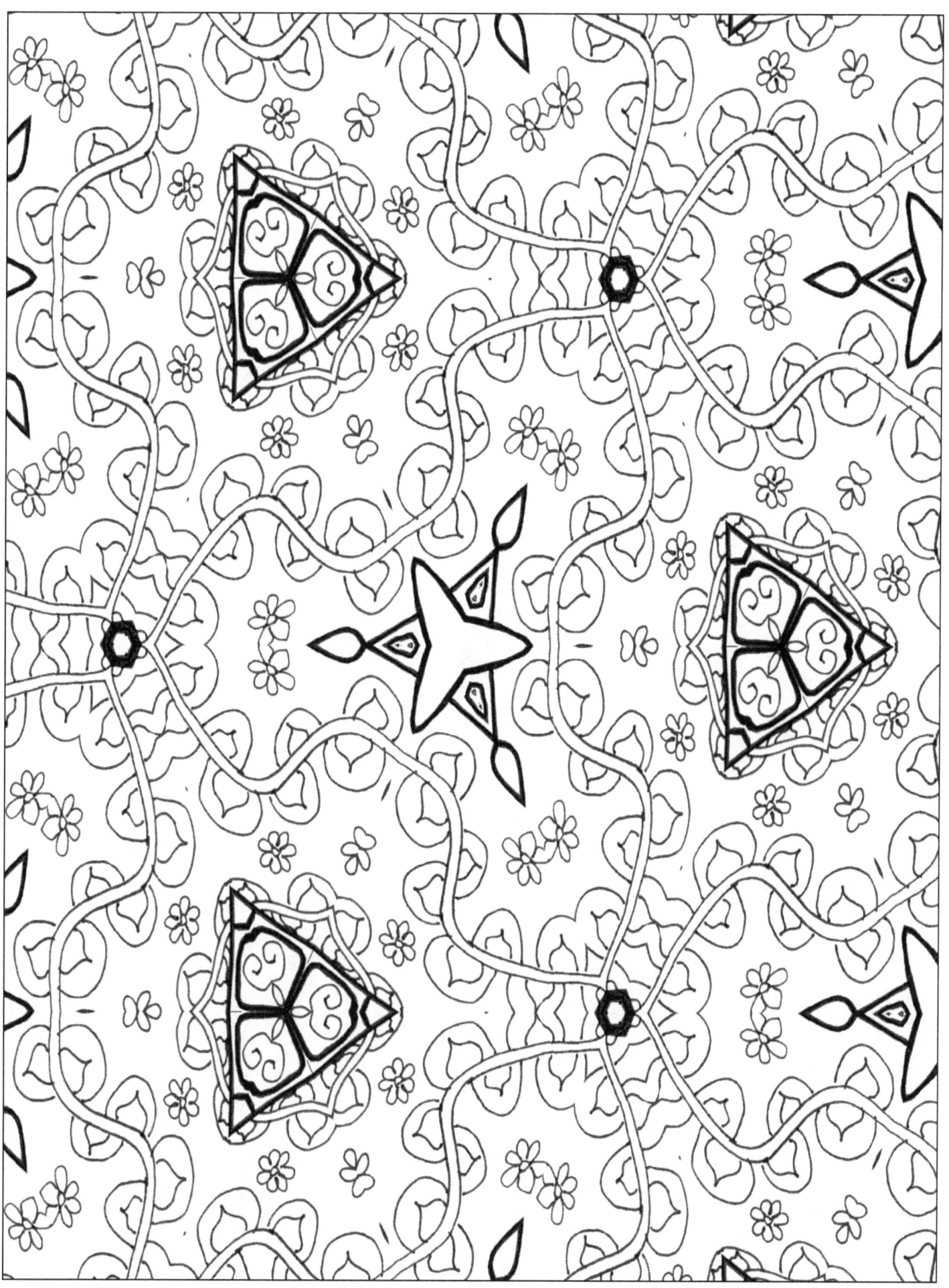

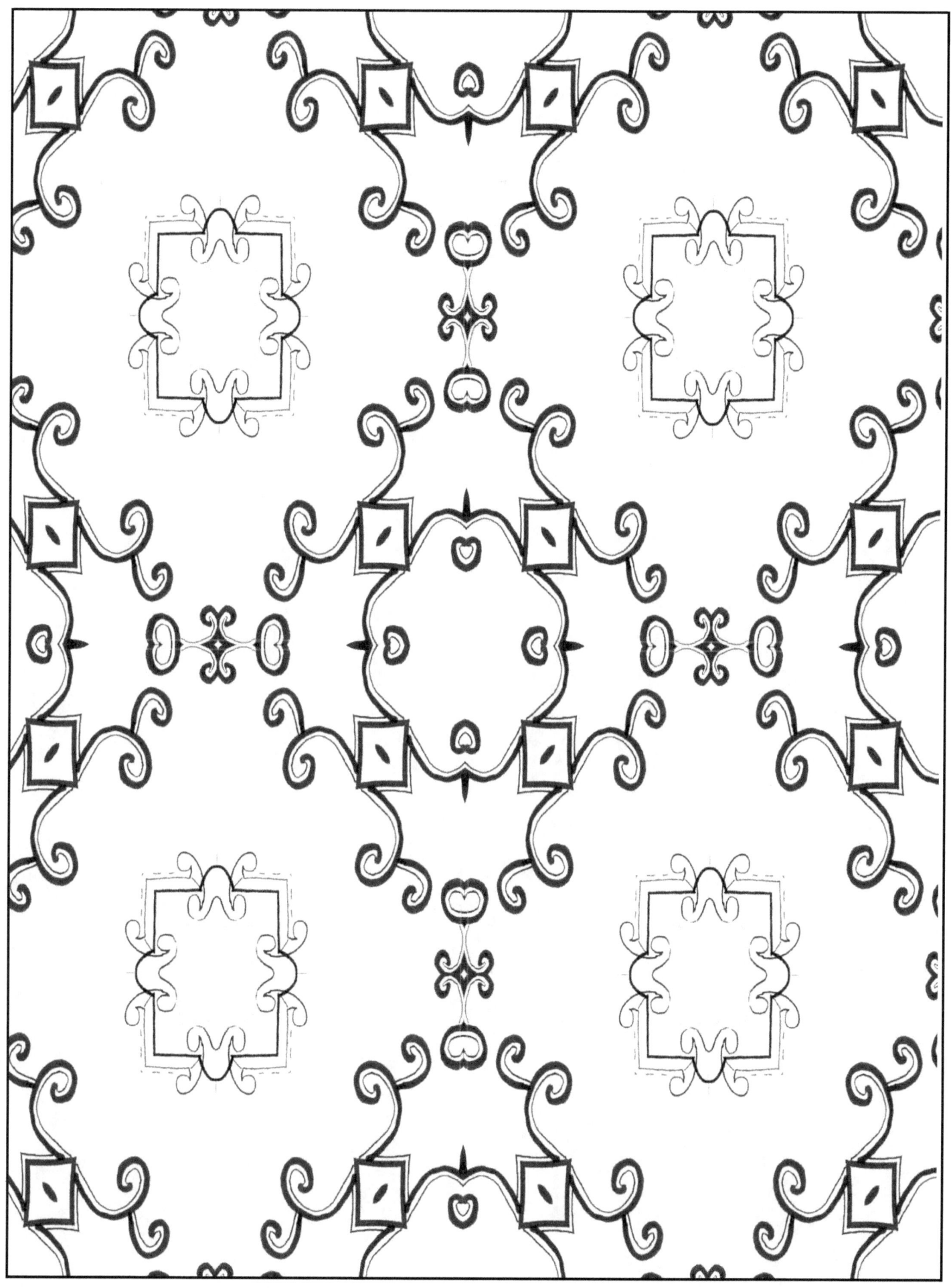

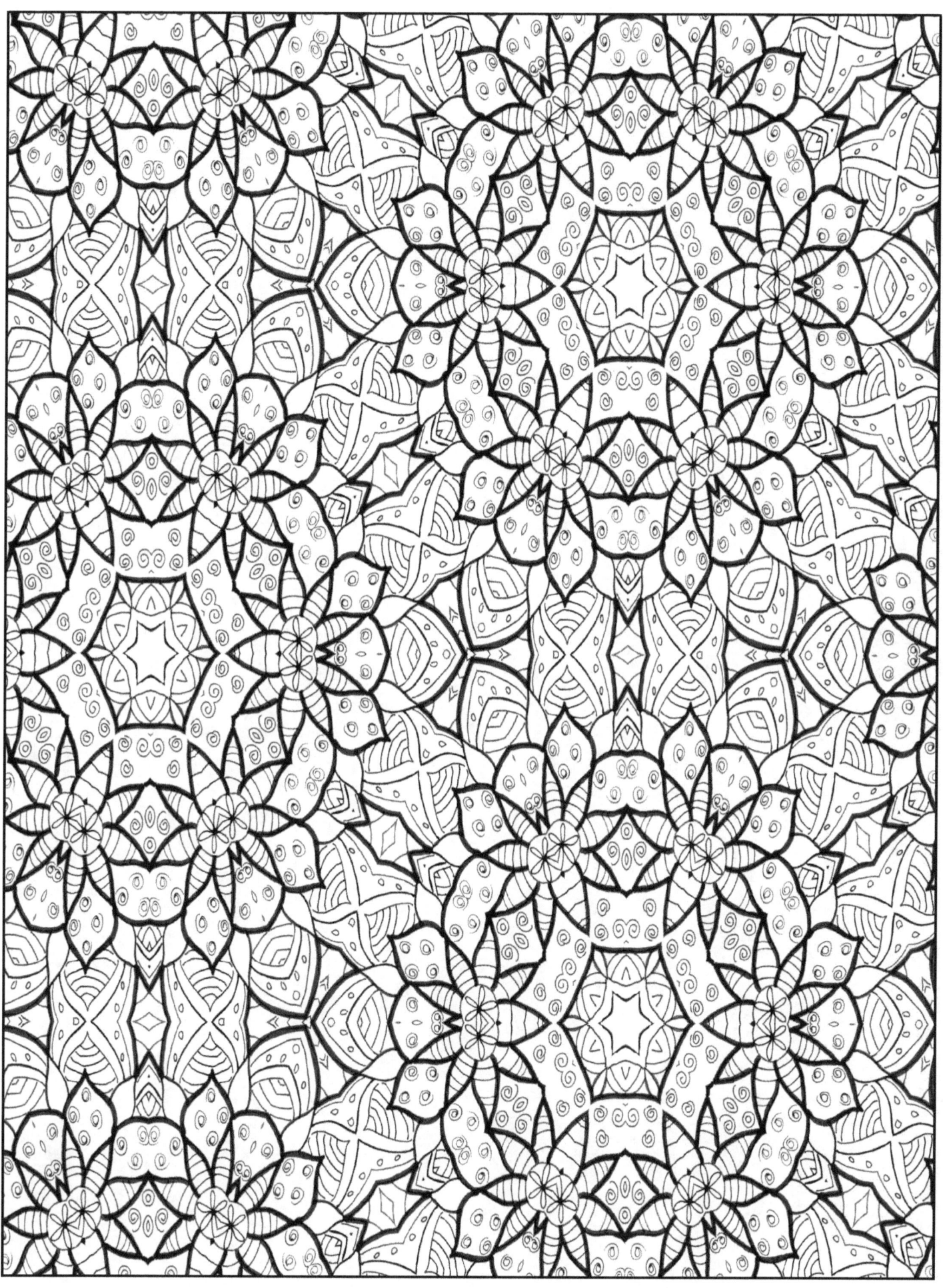

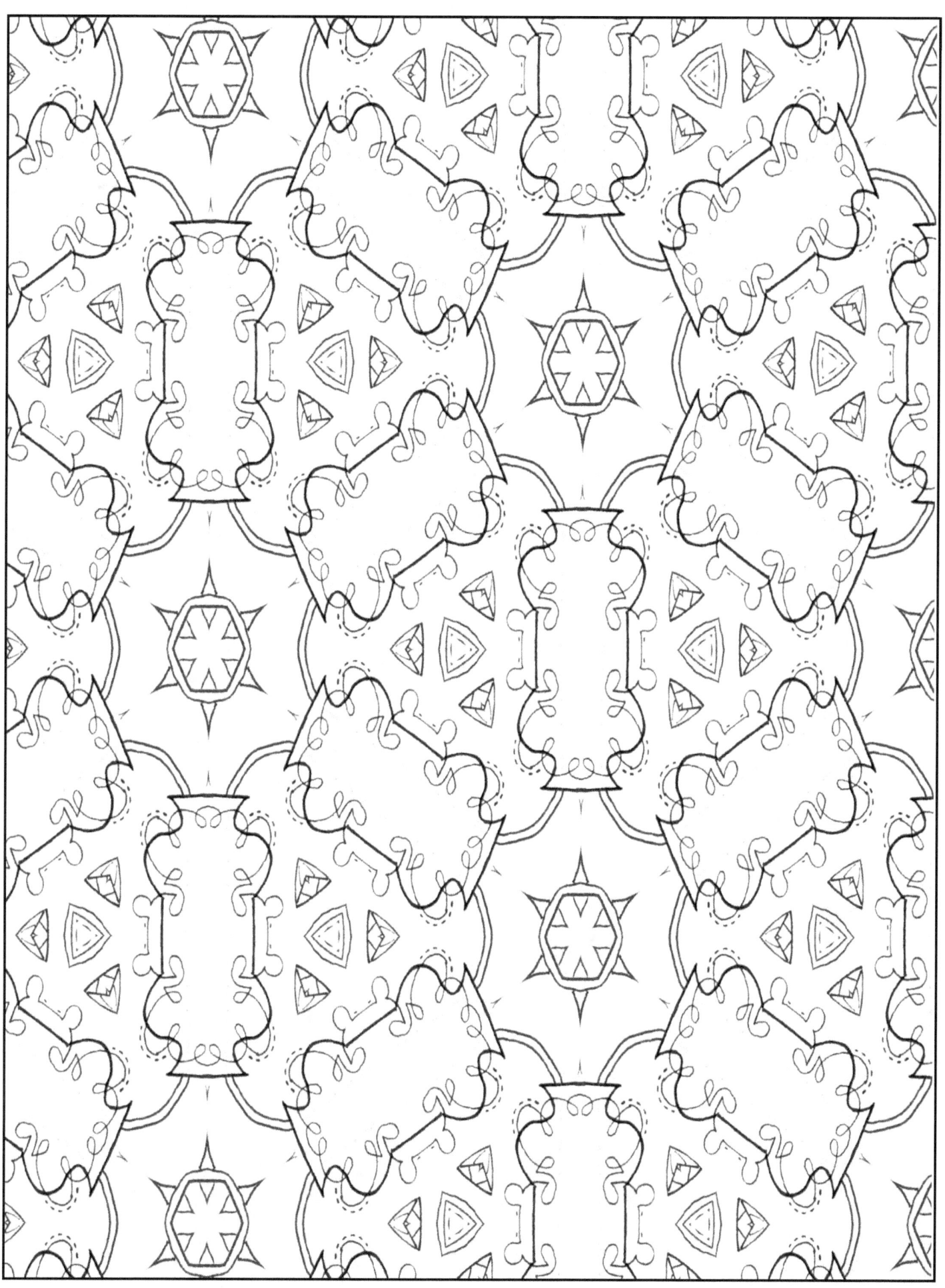

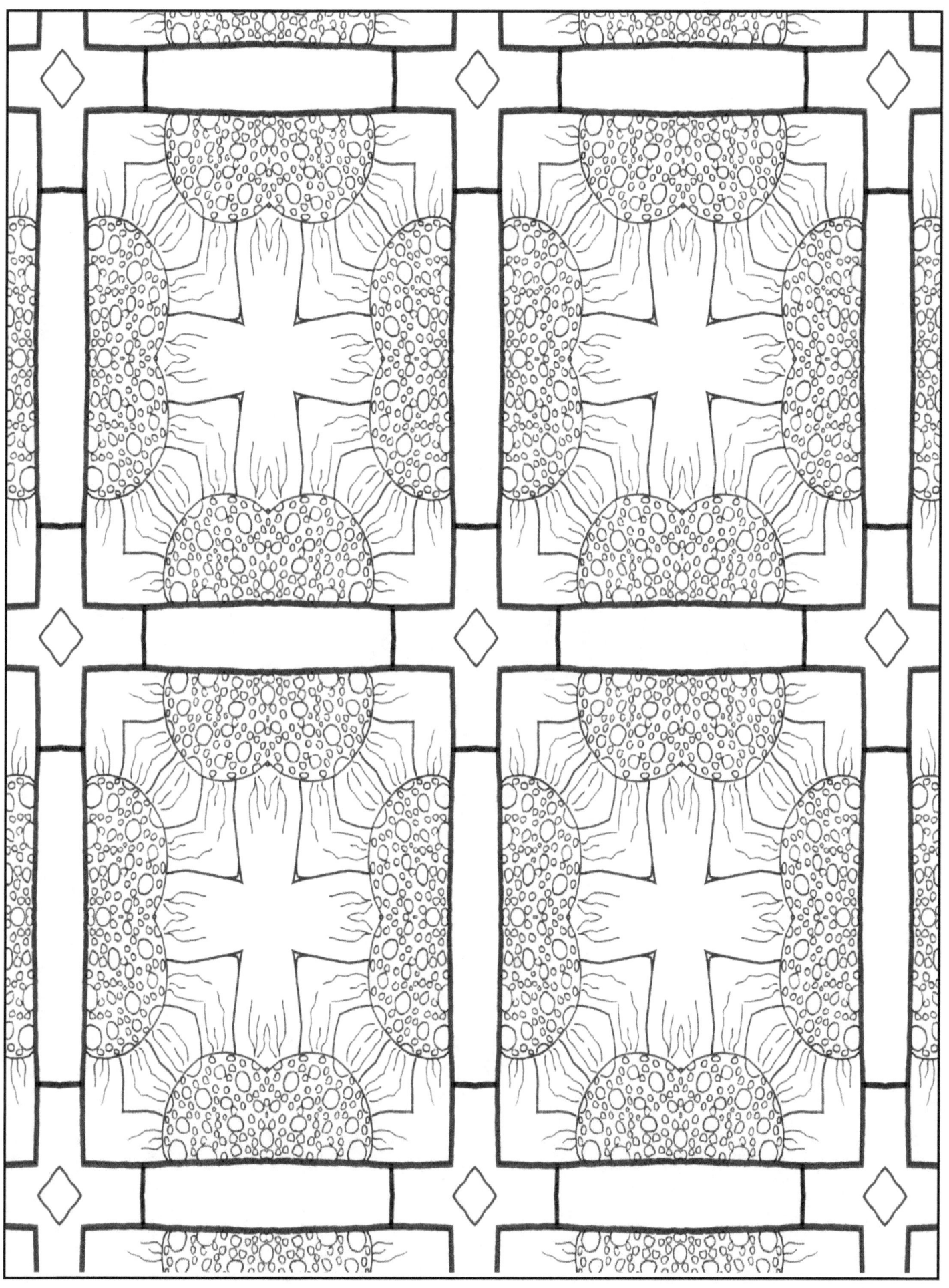

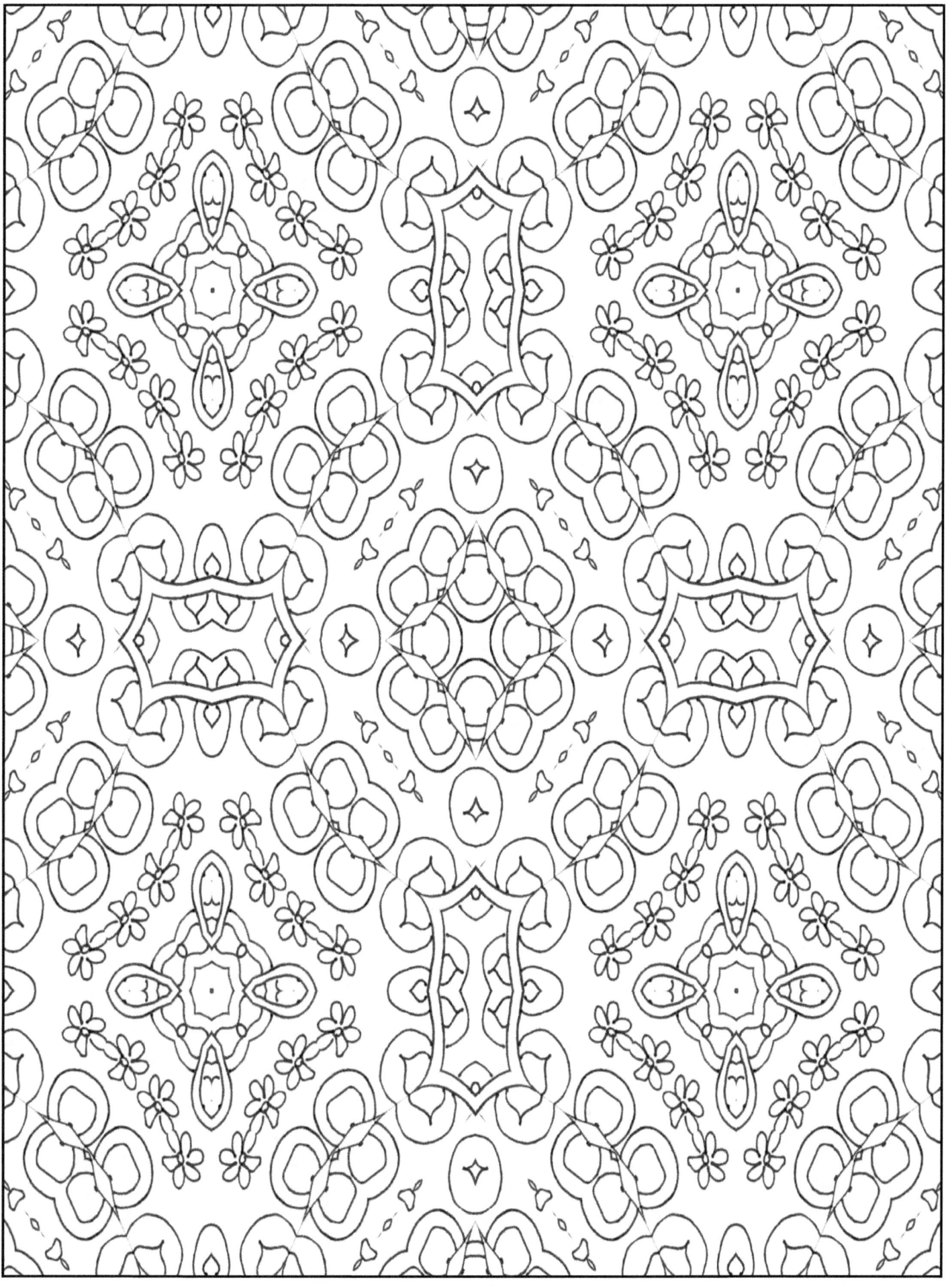

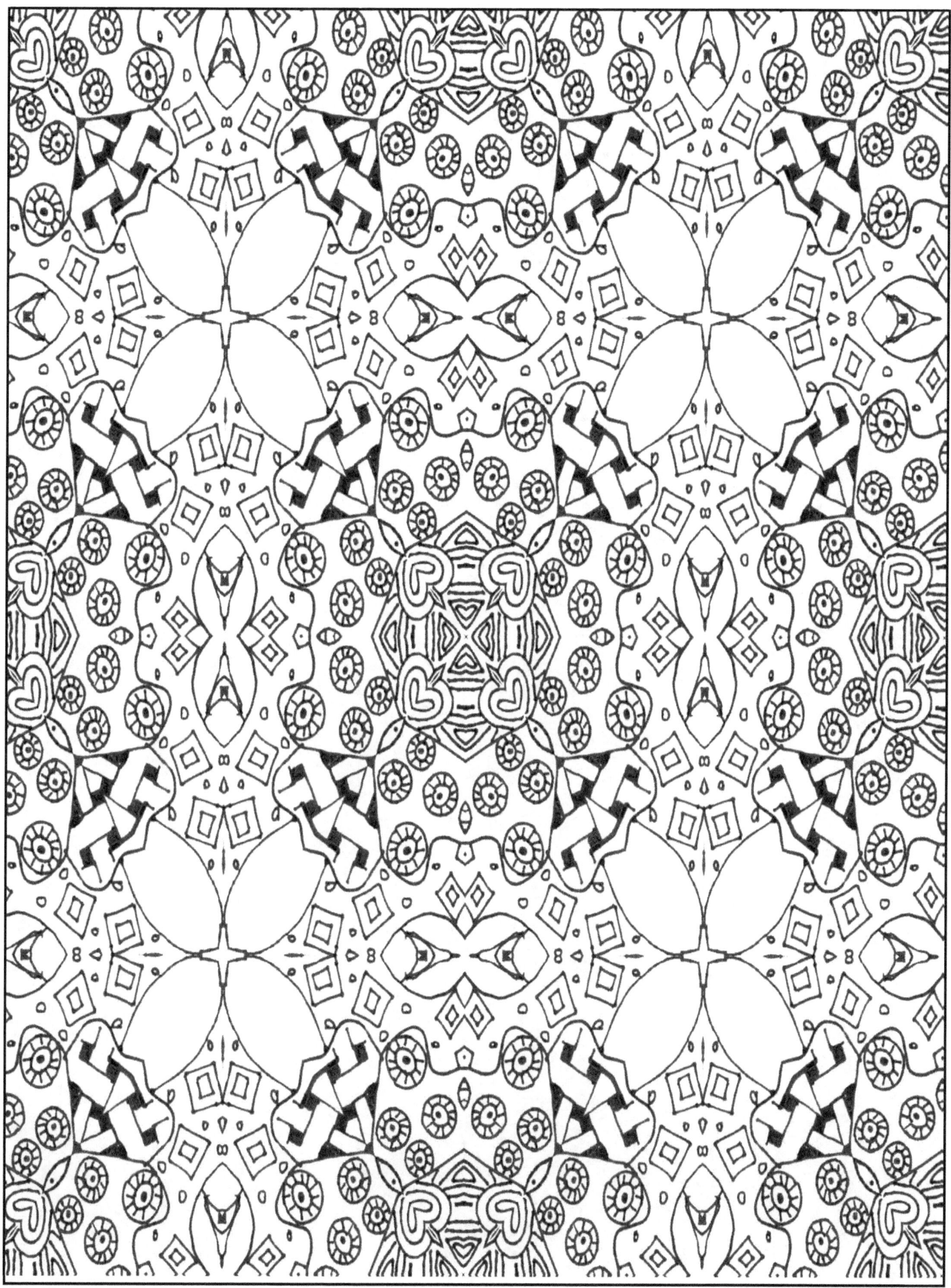

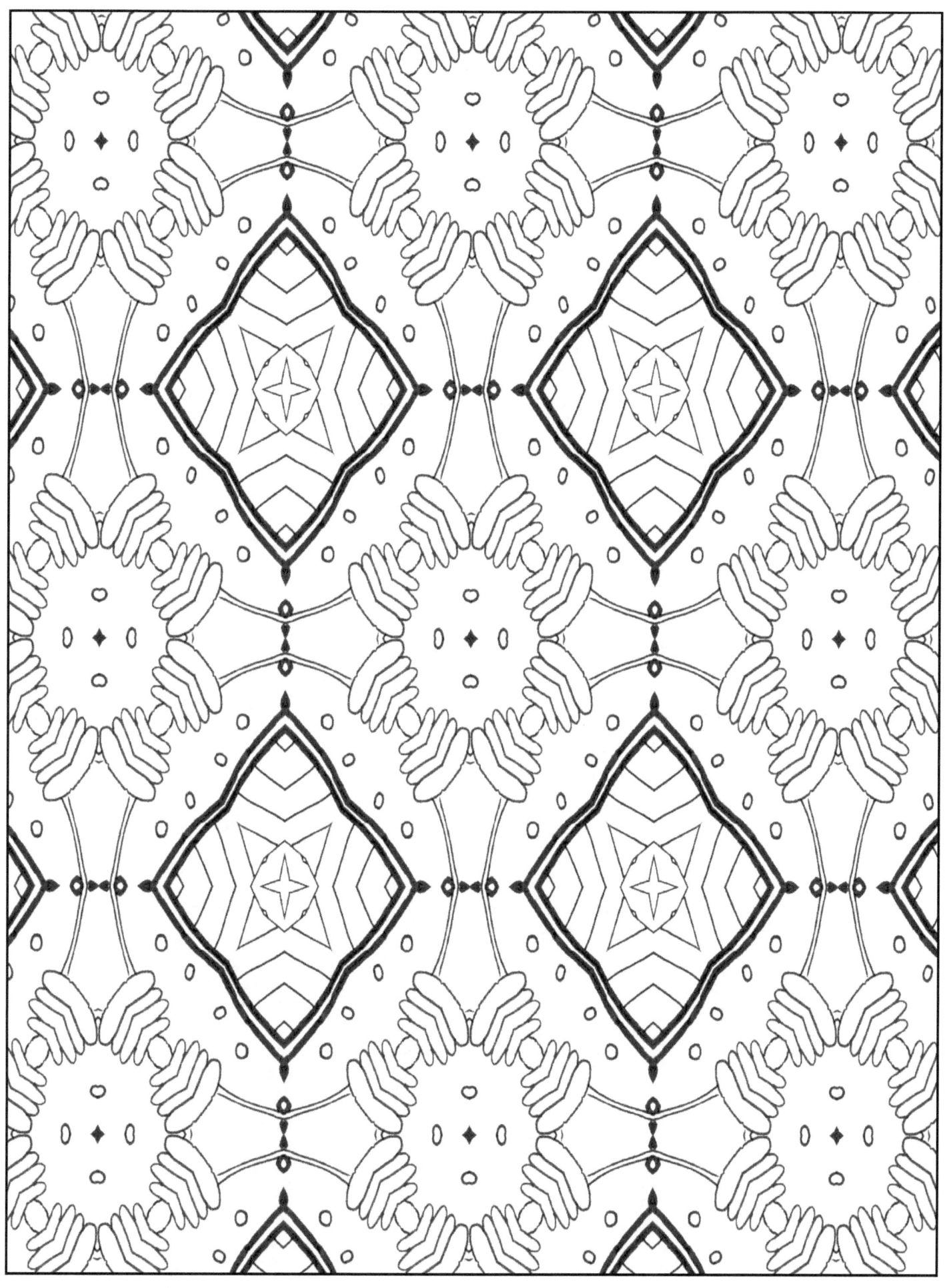

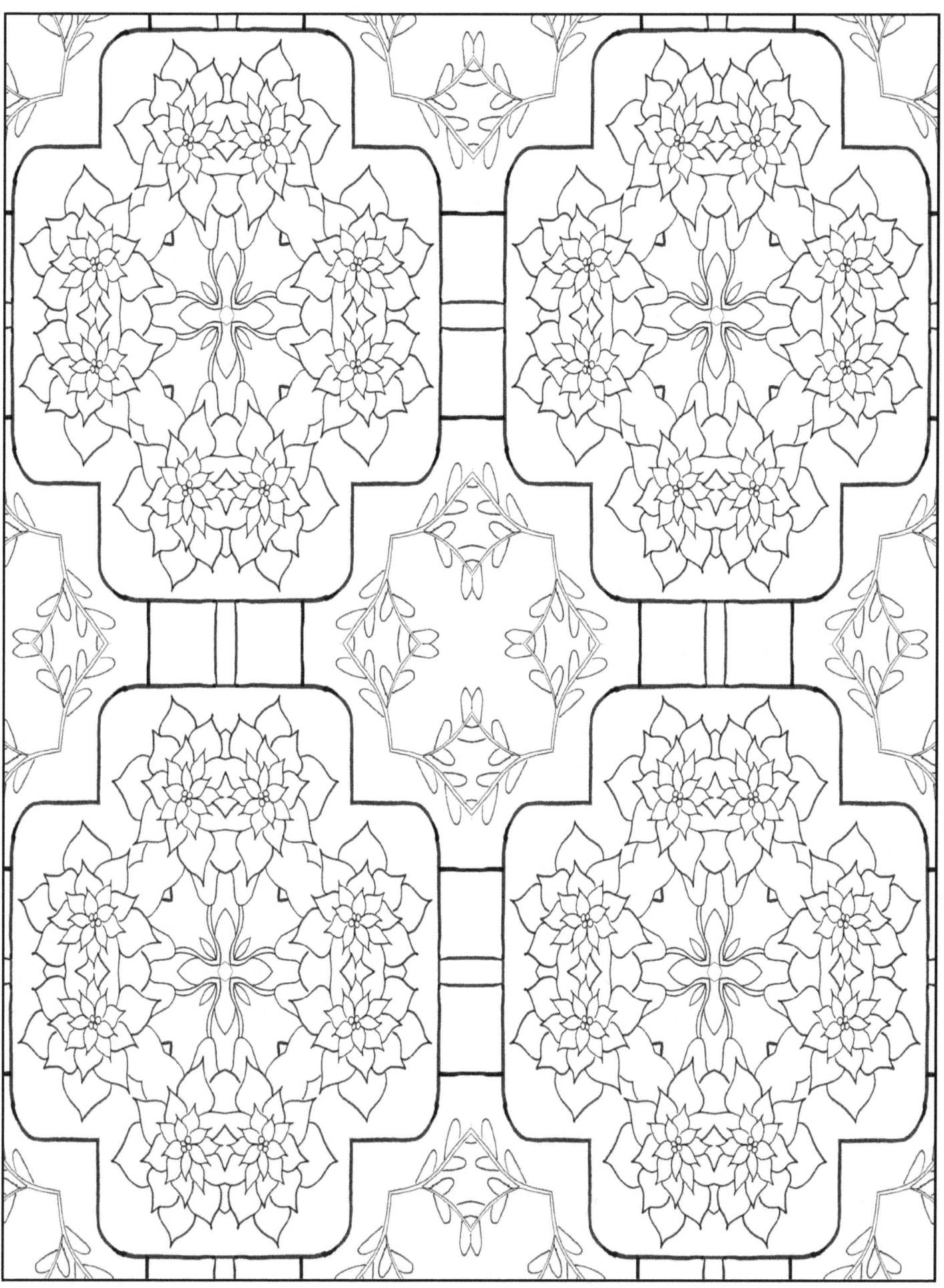

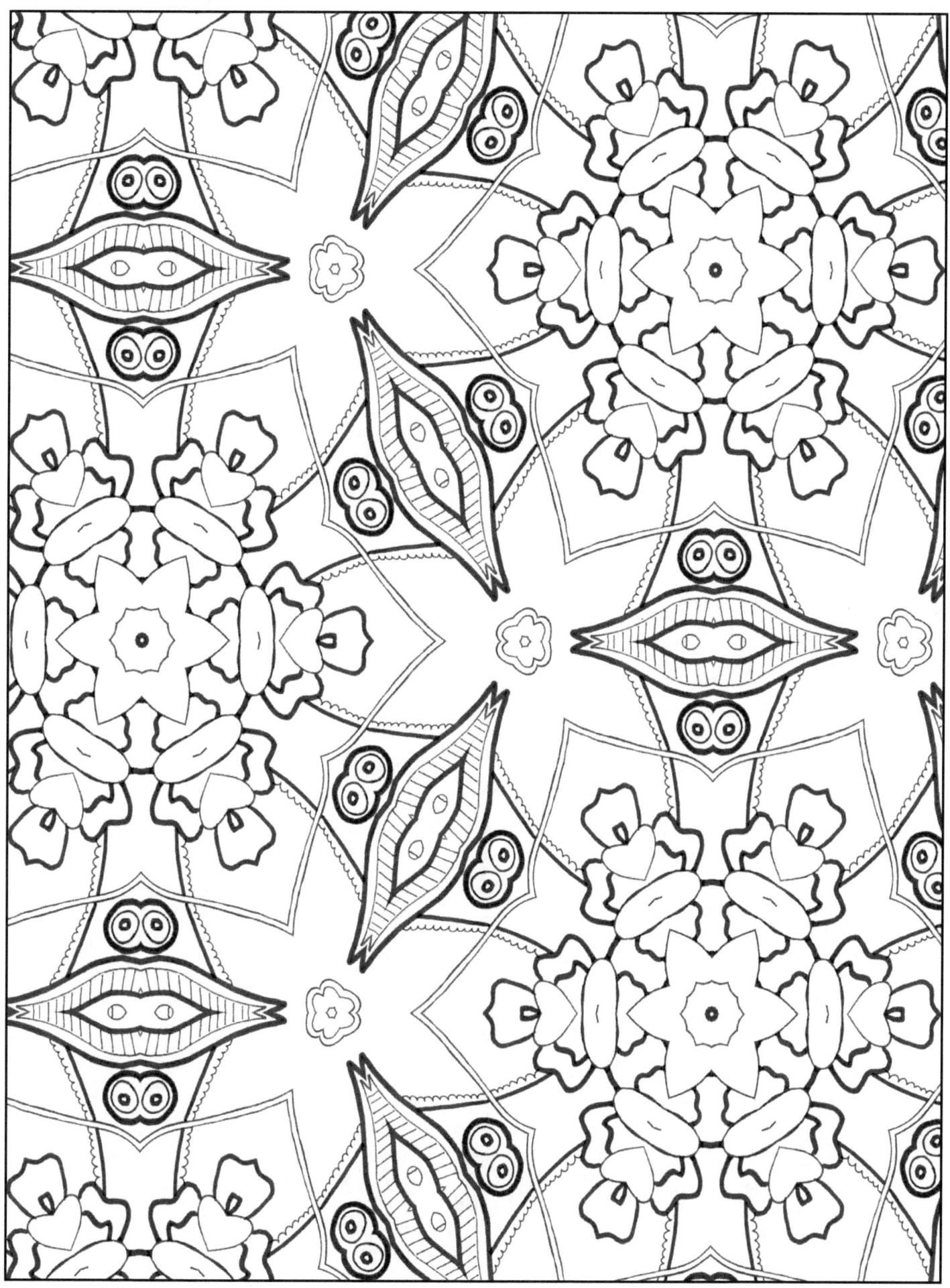

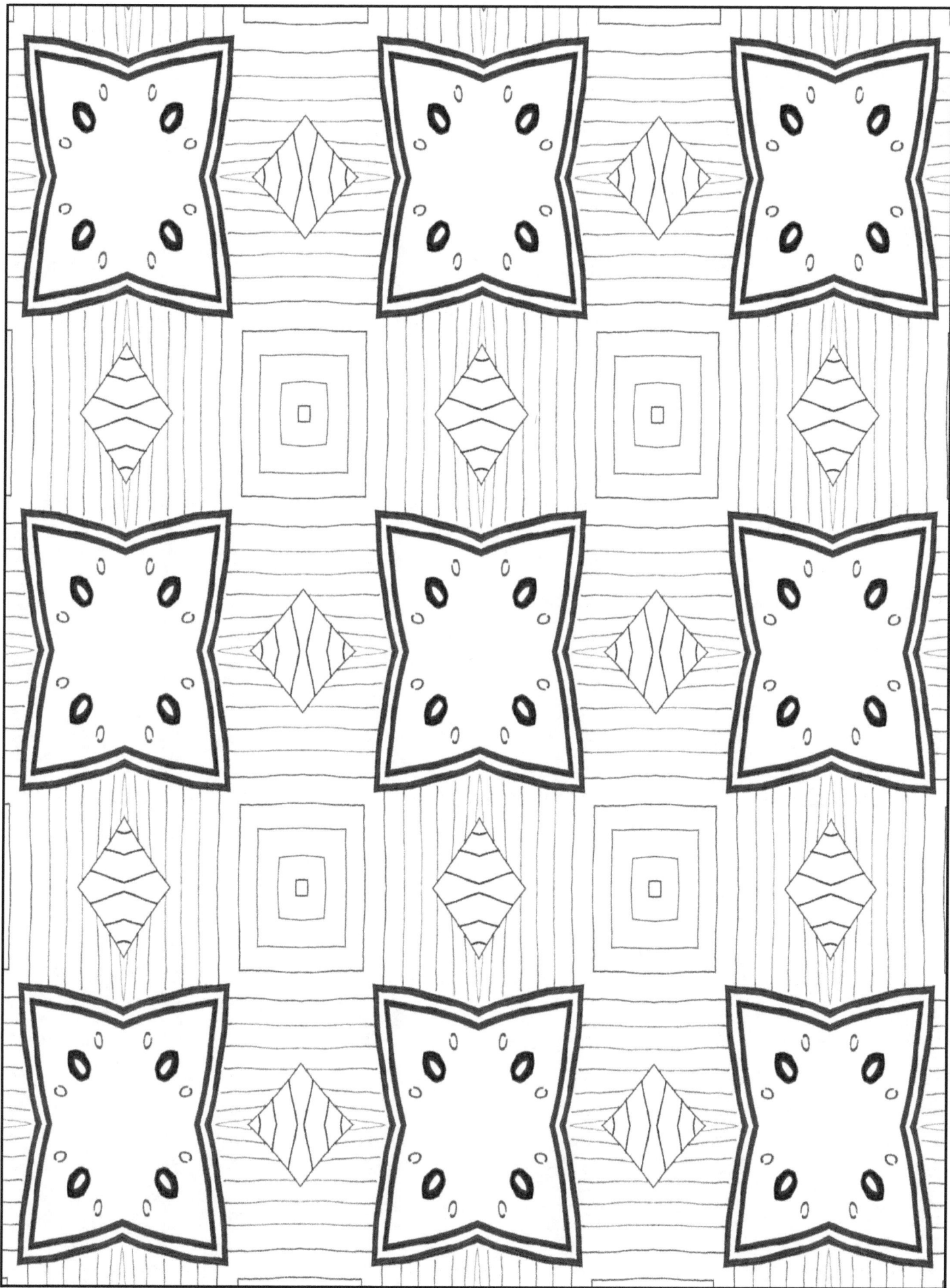

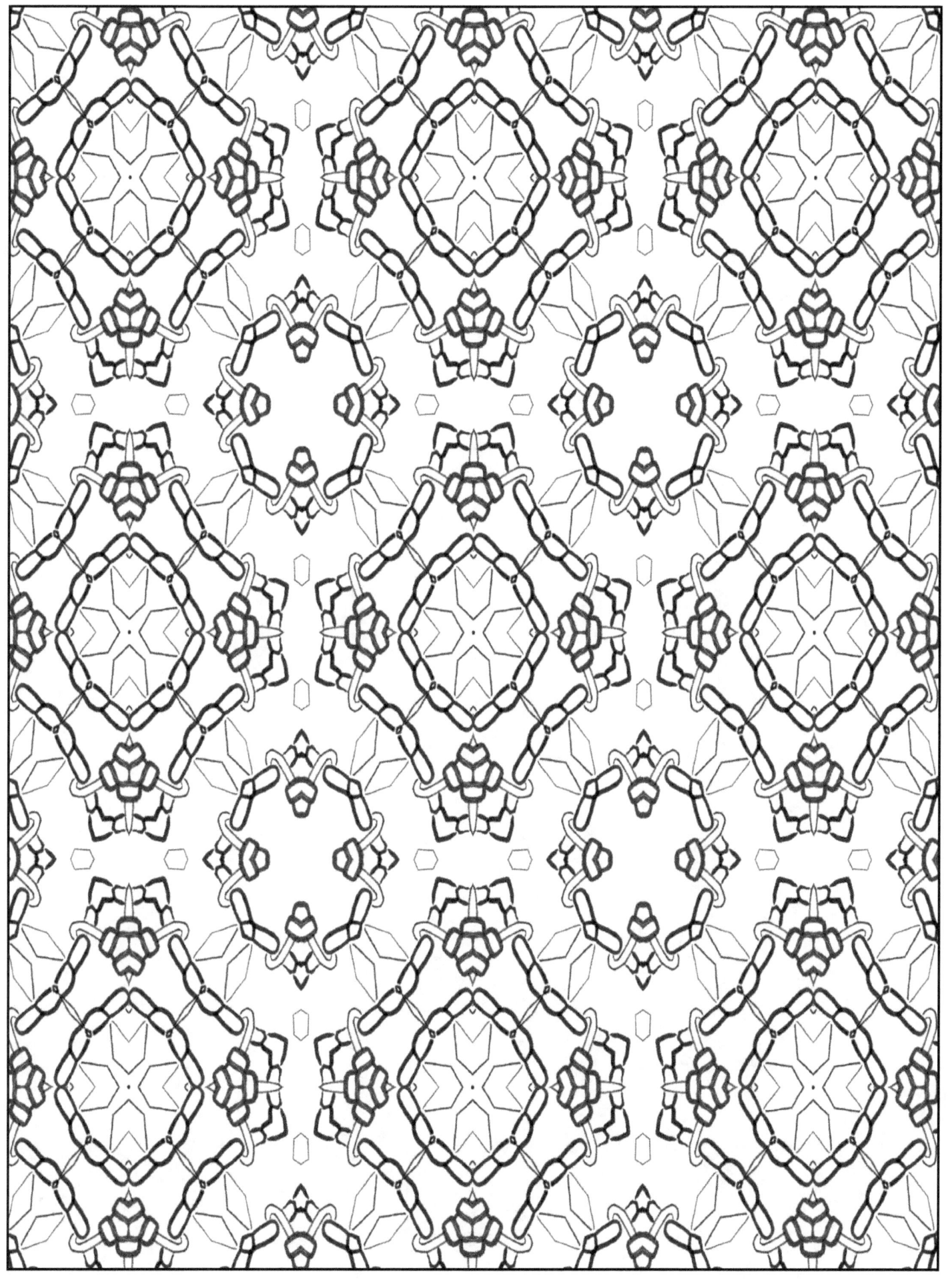

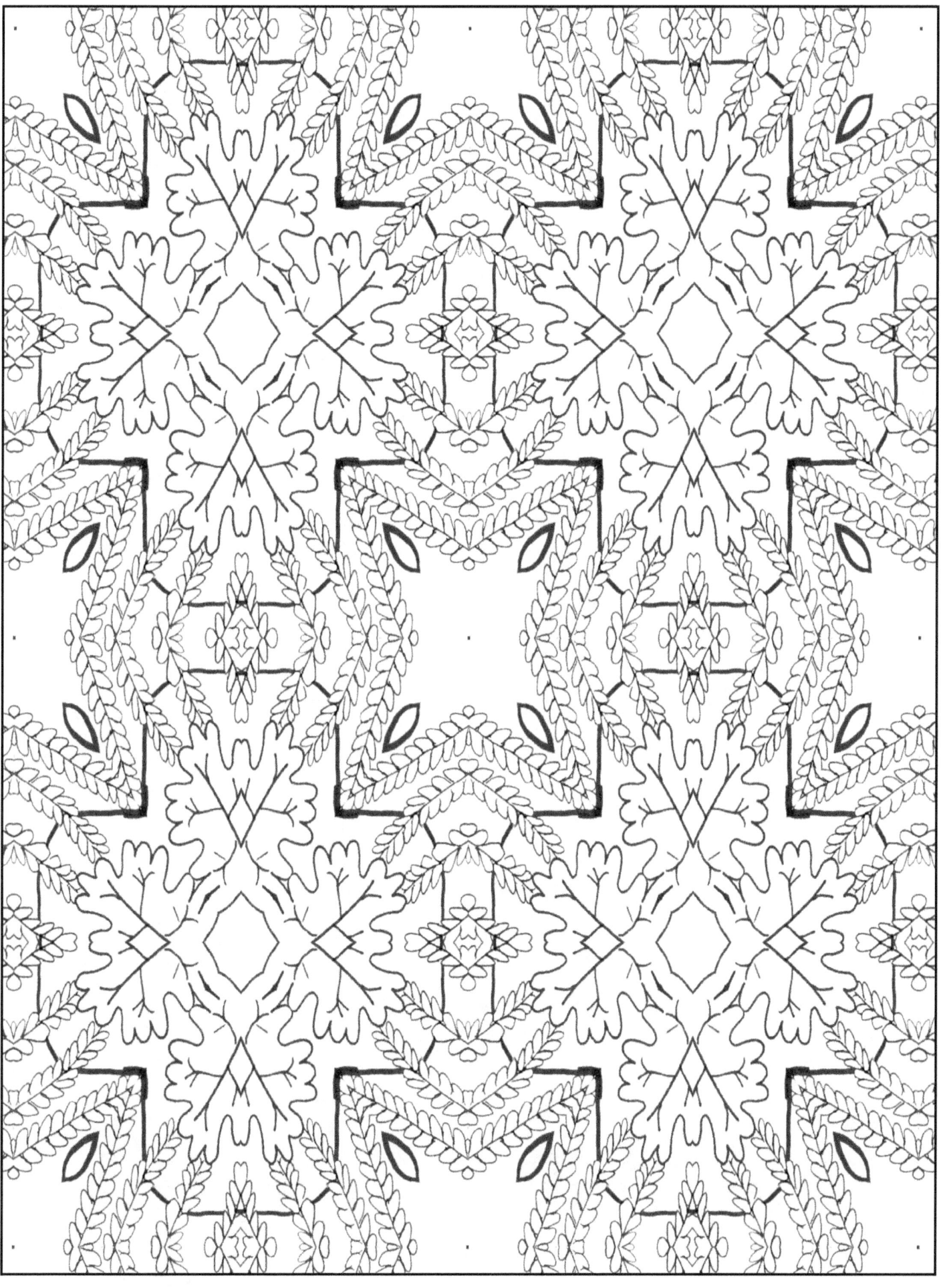

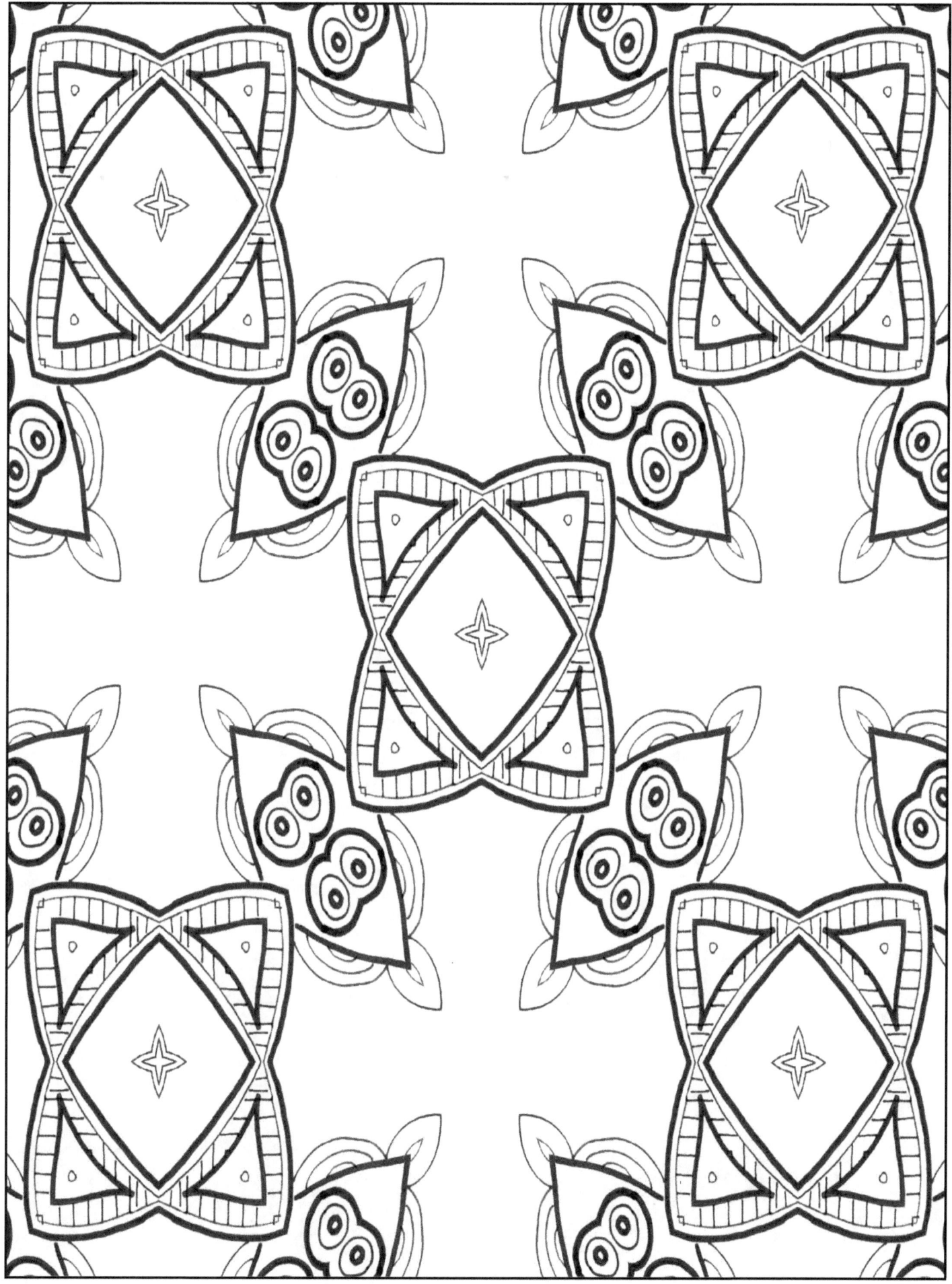

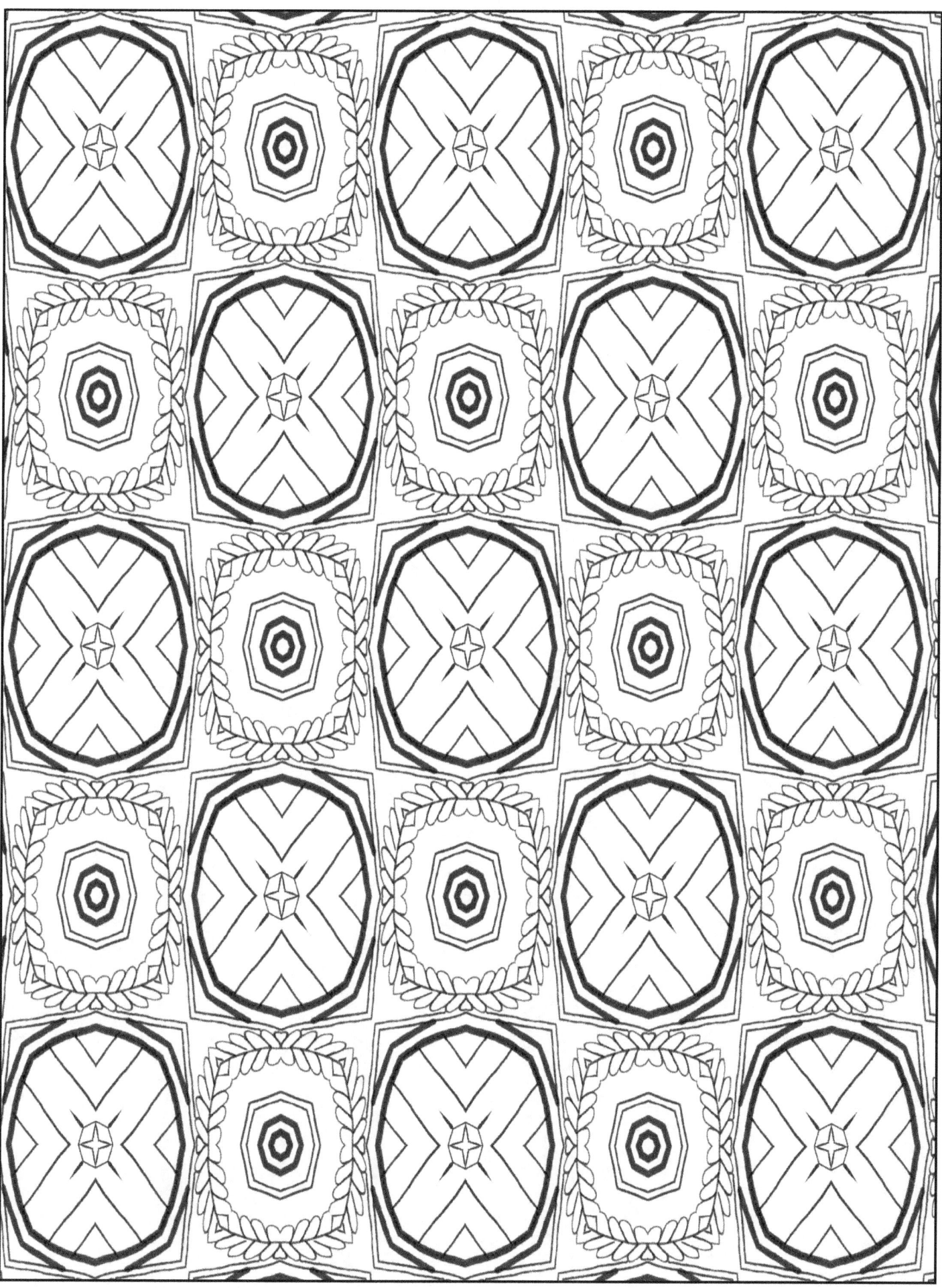

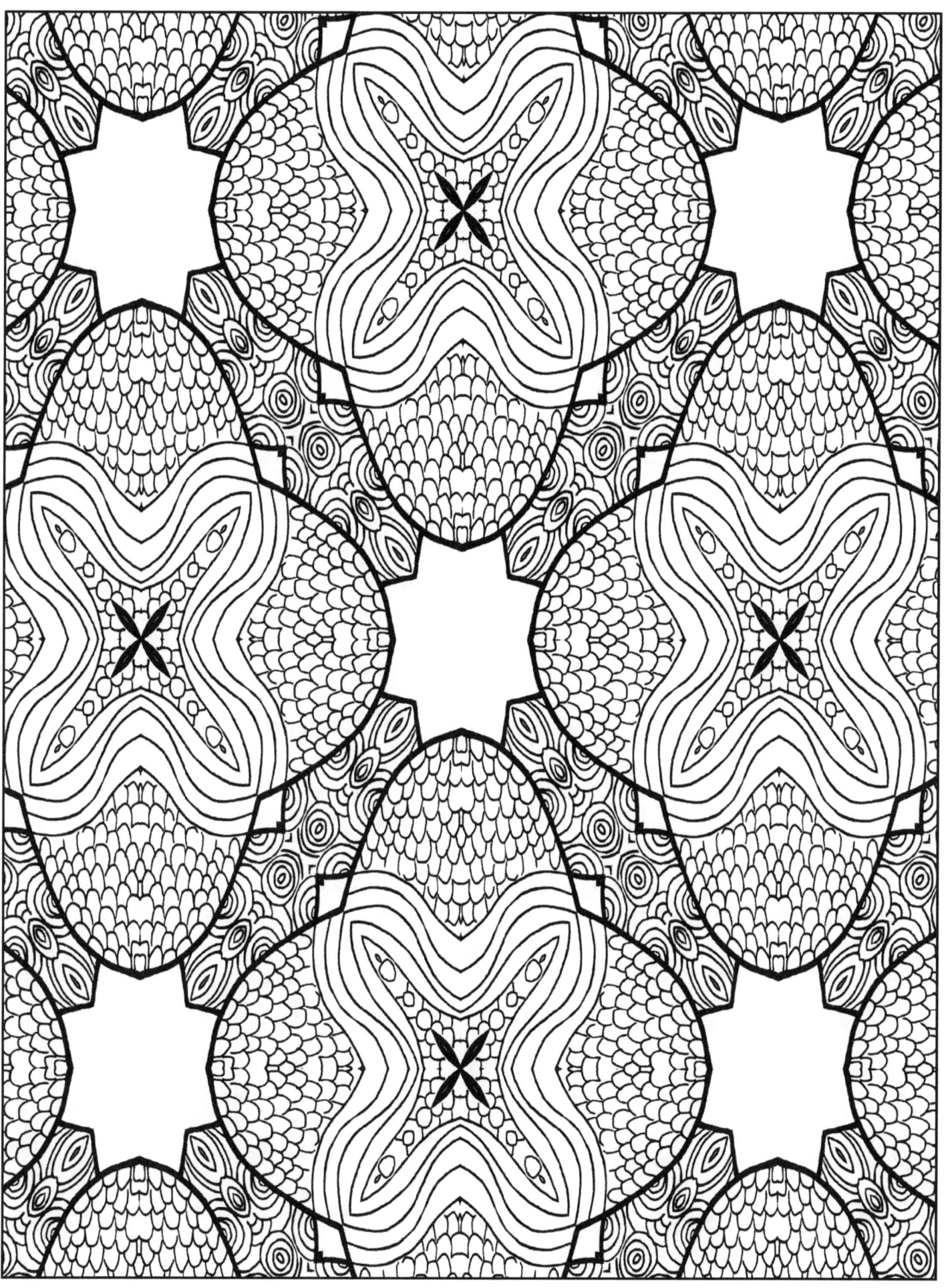

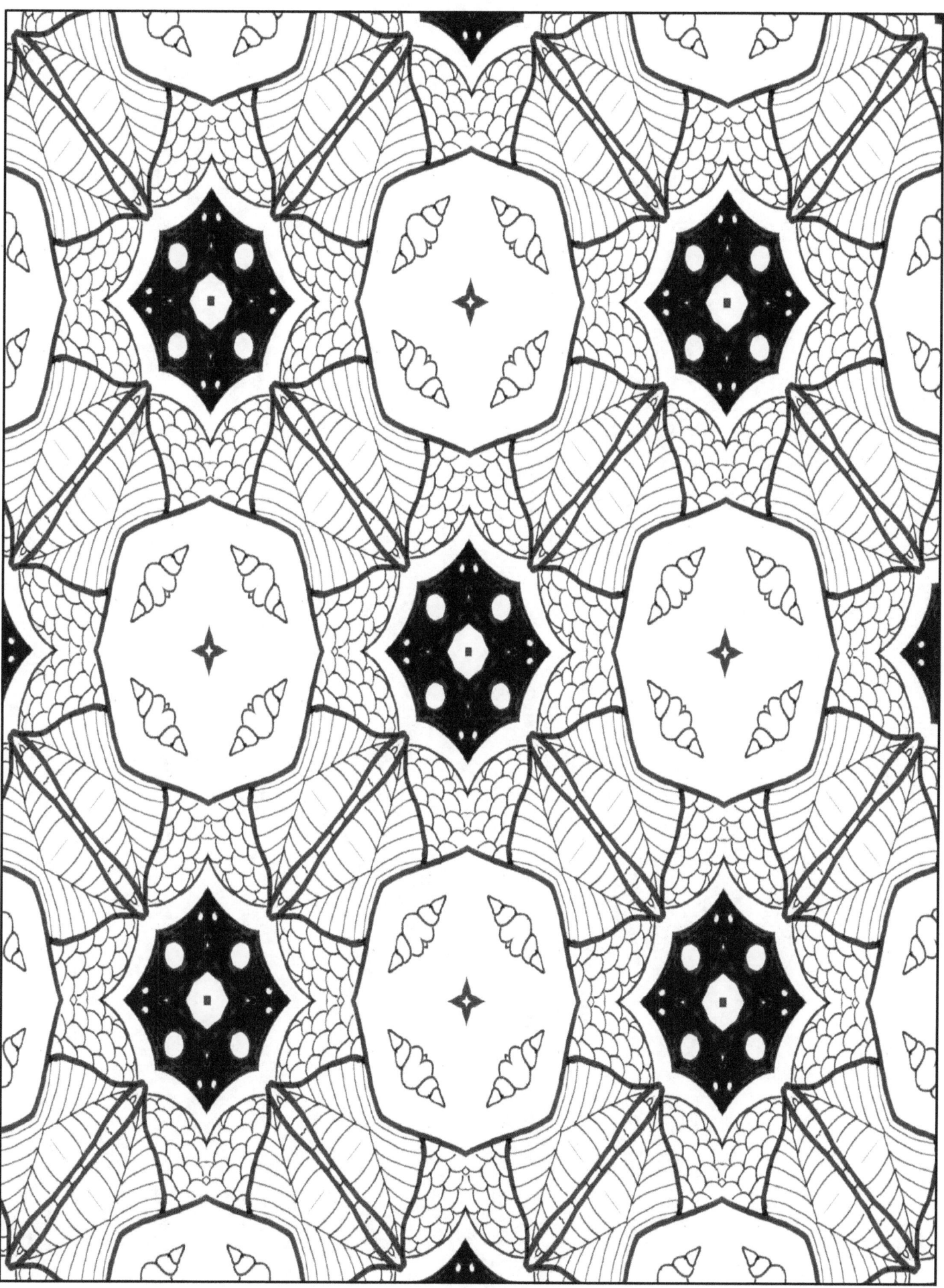

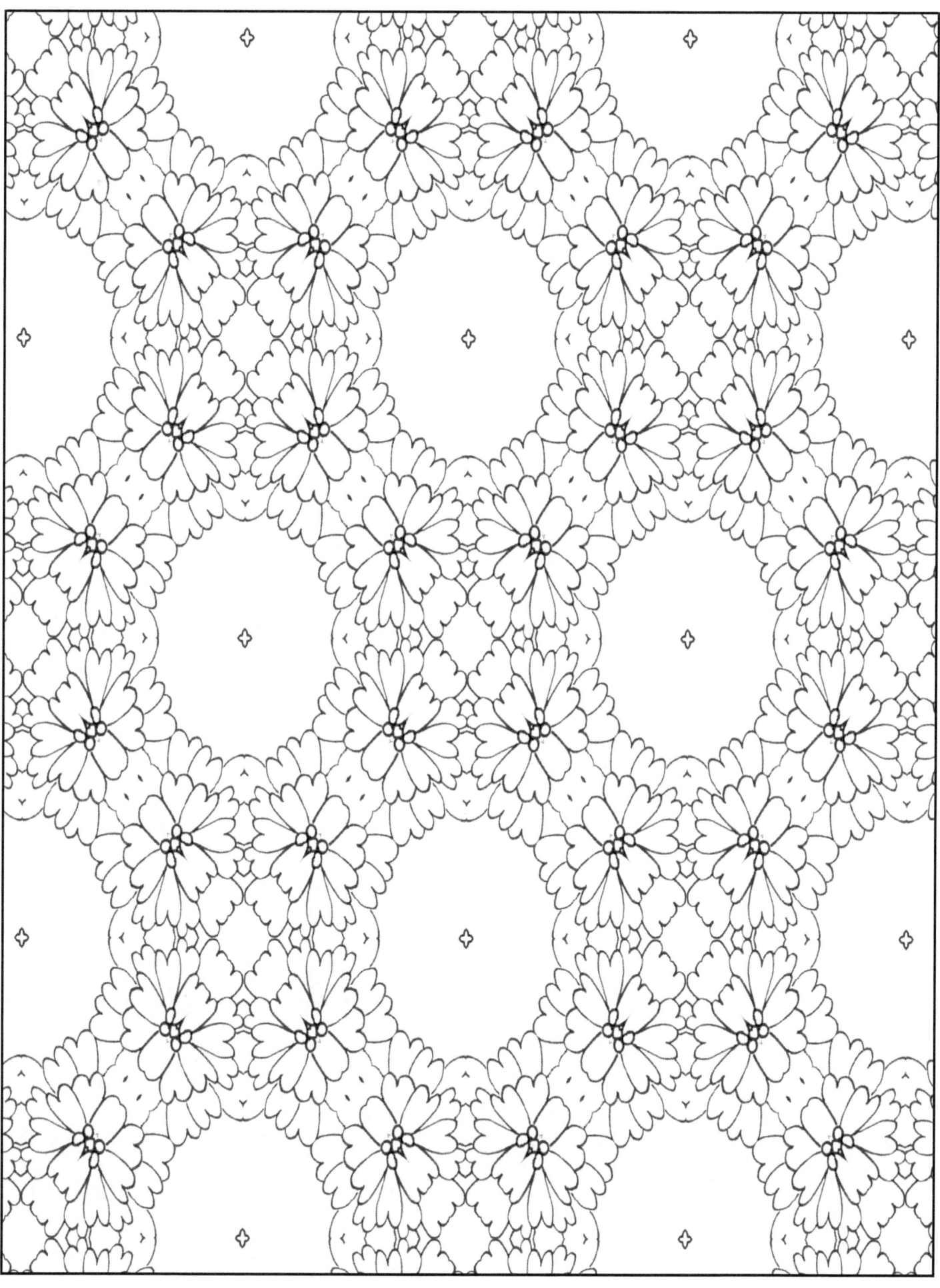

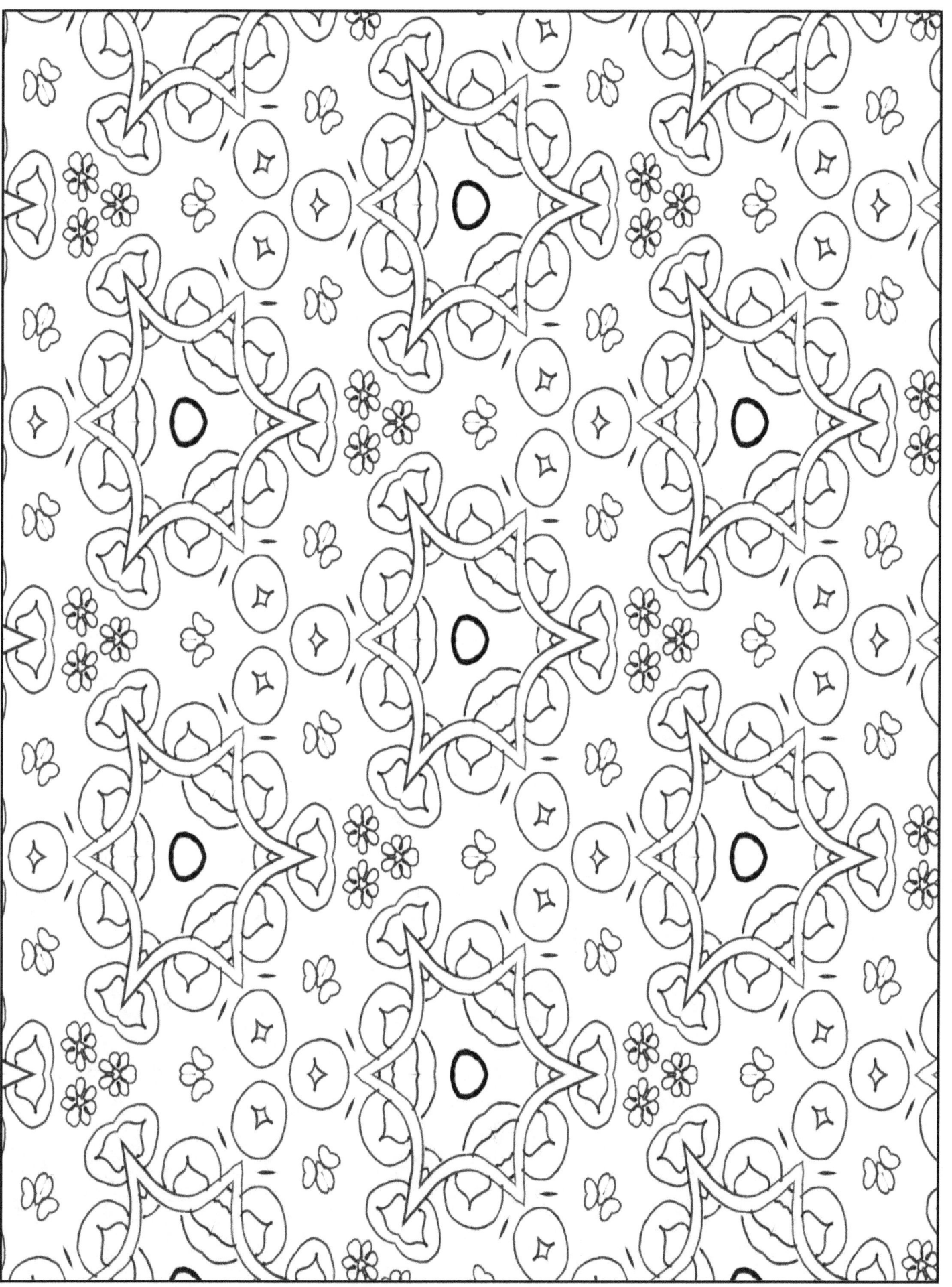

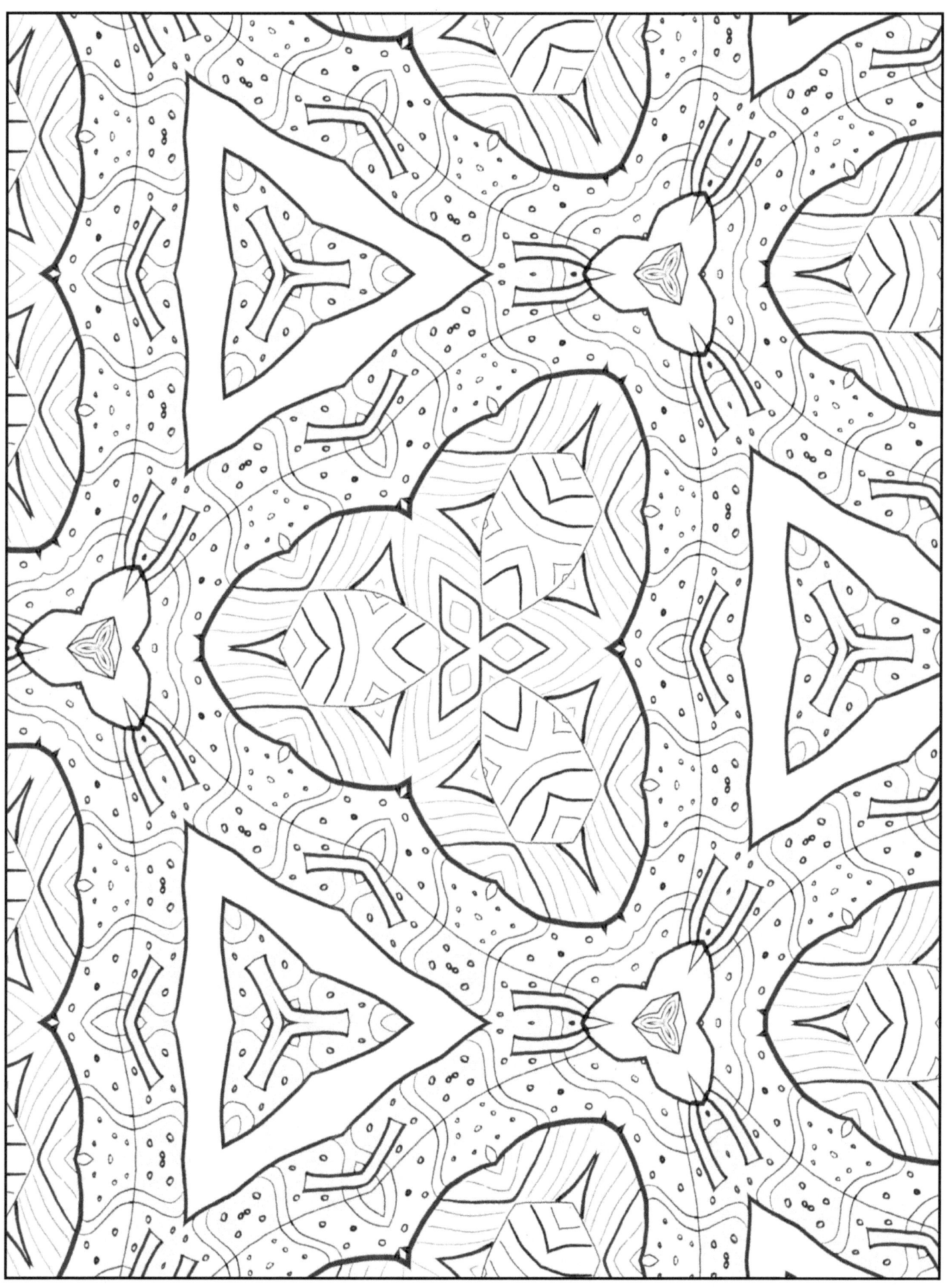

Bonus Pages

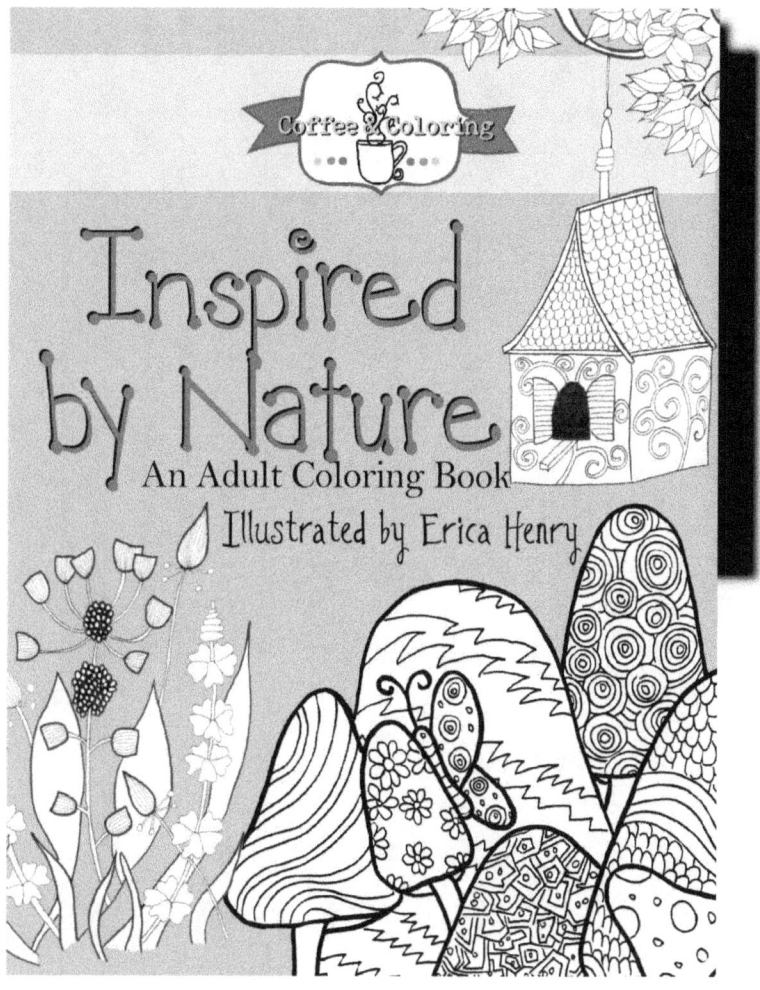

From Inspired by Nature

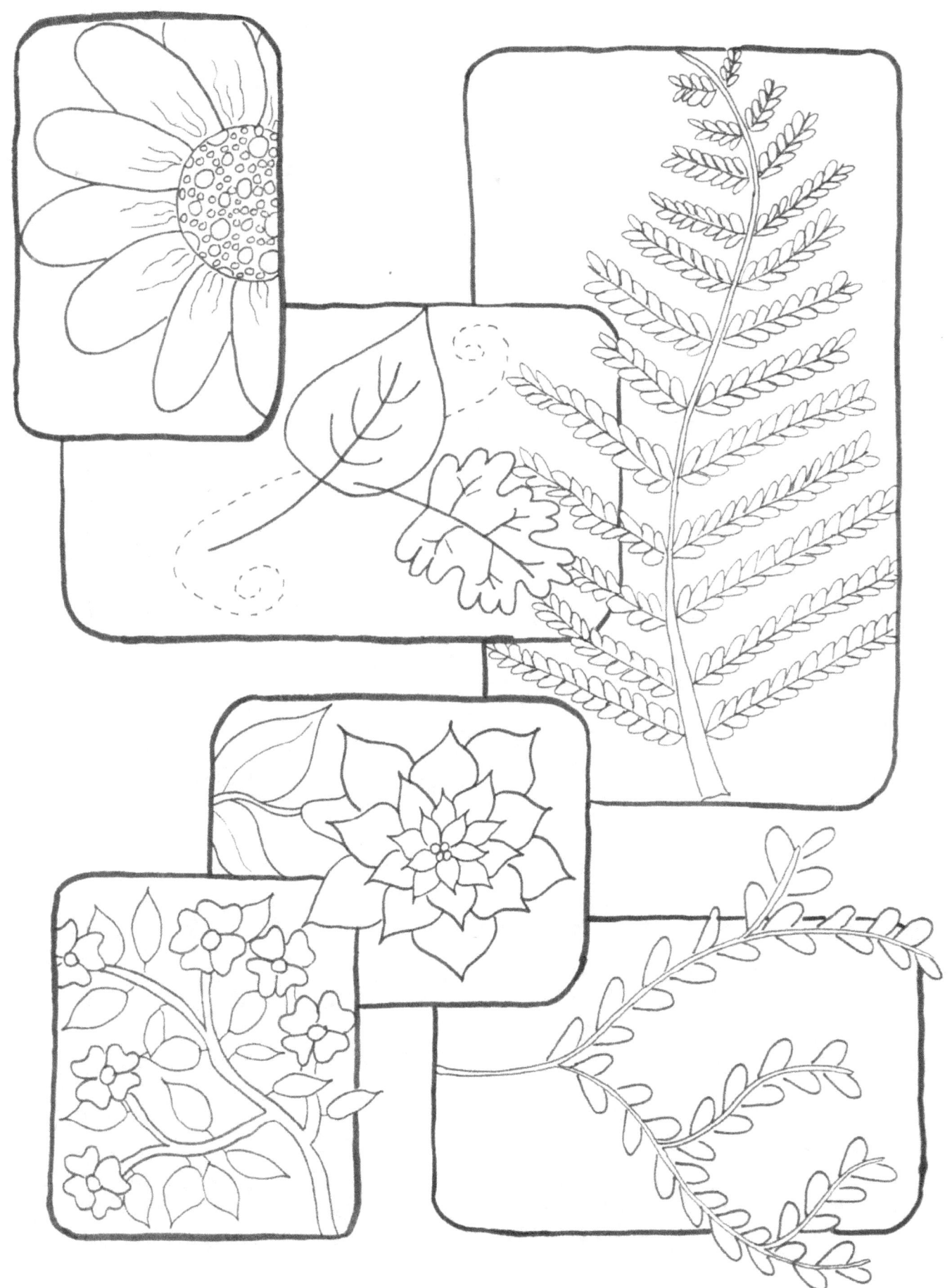

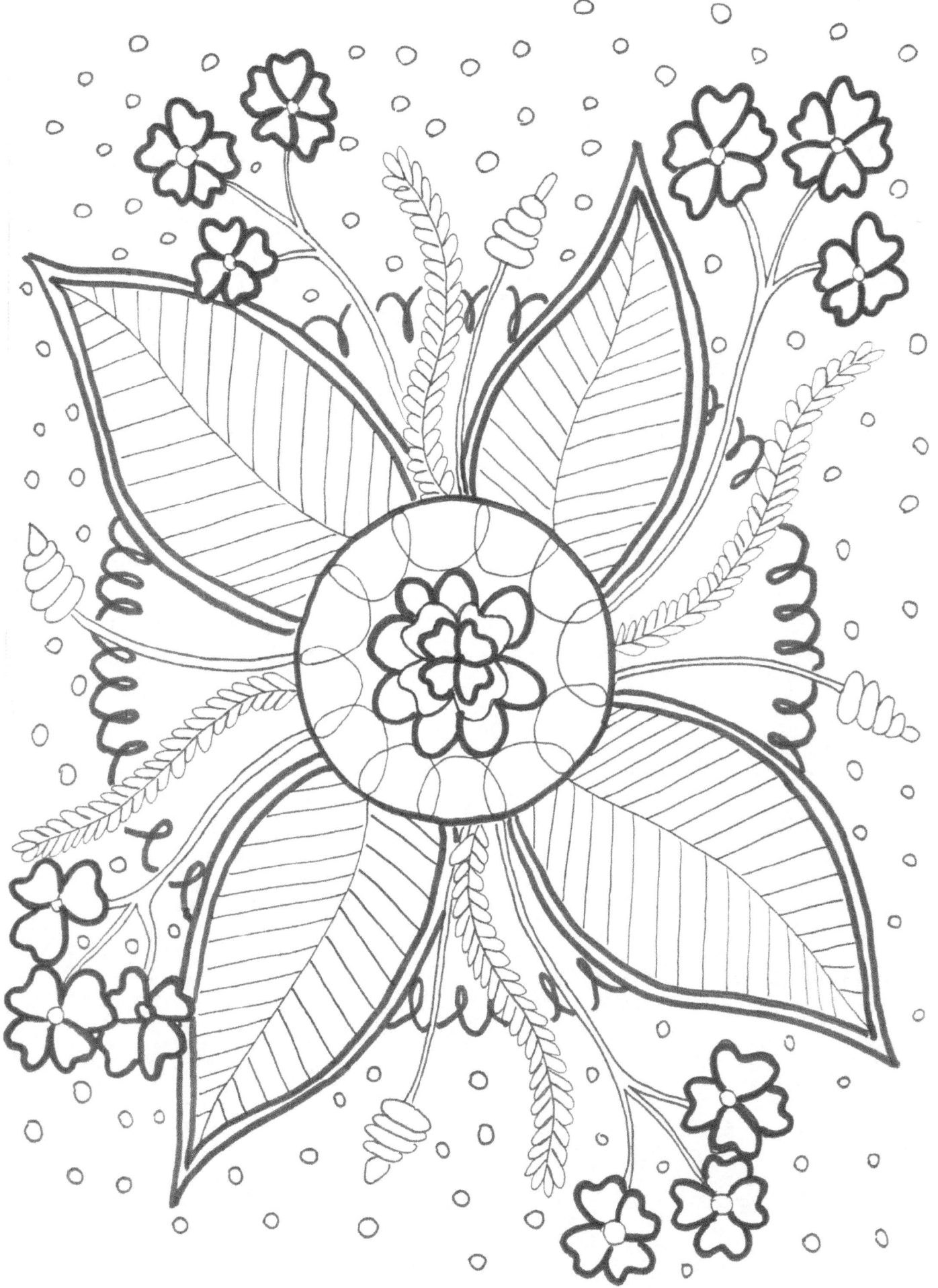

B & M Potterycrafts.

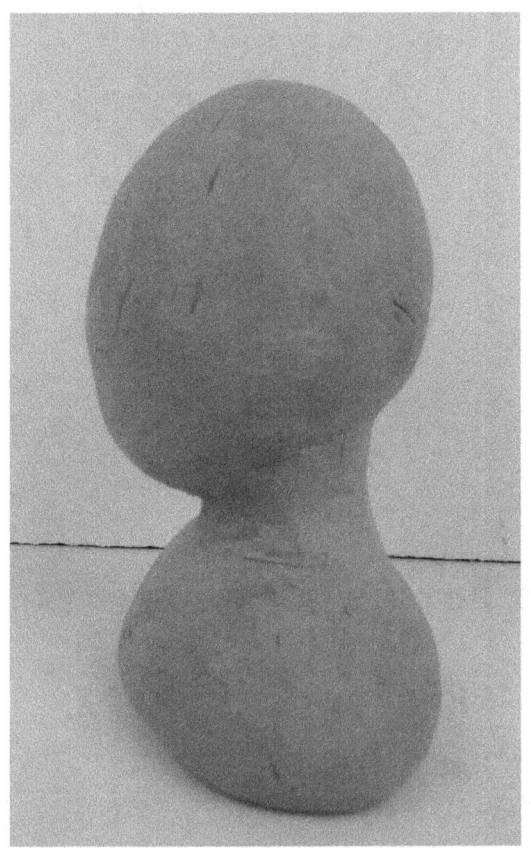

Clay modelling projects.

Double Thumb Pot Head.

Create the model shown on this cover by following step by step, easy to understand, instructions supported by still photos at each stage.

Brian Rollins.

B & M Potterycrafts.

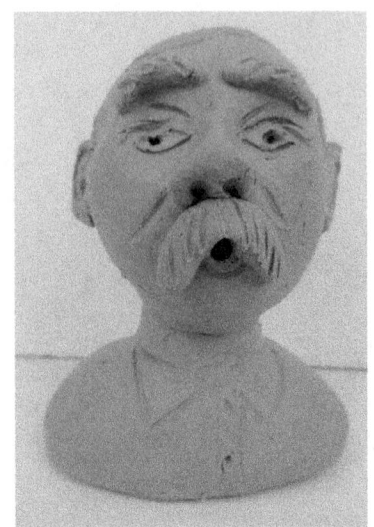

Double Thumb Pot Head. Contents and sequence.

Prepare the clay.

Make an irregular thumb pot.

Make a second pot.

Join two thumb pots.

Make the shoulders.

Make and fit the neck.

Join head to shoulders.

Decorate and detail the model.

Worksheet.

Double Thumb Pot Head.

Prepare the clay.

Roll the clay between the palms of your hands,

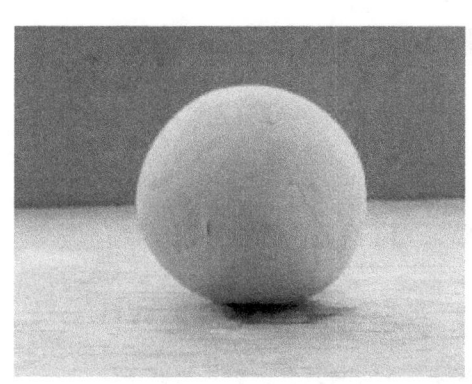

exerting sufficient force to remove any lumps or bumps. Don't be tempted to take the easy route to smooth the clay by rolling it on the wooden work surface as this removes

moisture from the clay and could make it too hard for modelling. Any creases or cracks can be smoothed using the fingers. Continue to roll the clay until the surface is smooth and the clay is the desired shape ie a ball shape.

Take the clay ball between the palms of your hands and roll it into an egg shape. Roll the clay backwards and forwards across your palms exerting sufficient pressure to form the egg shape. The best way is to roll the clay a few times, check the shape then roll it a bit more, keep

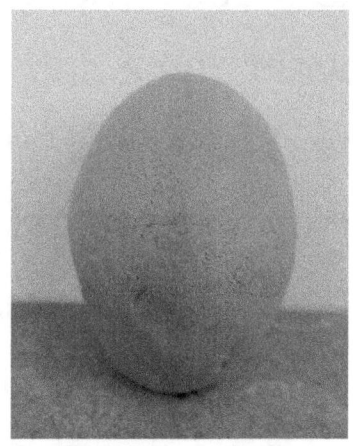

rolling and checking until you get the shape that you

need. Complete the shape by rounding off the ends of the egg with your fingers.

Make an oval (irregular) thumb pot.

By irregular thumb pots I mean any thumb pot which does not start with a sphere of clay or does not finish as a spherical shape.

The requirement for an oval shape rather than a round or spherical one is that very few figures which

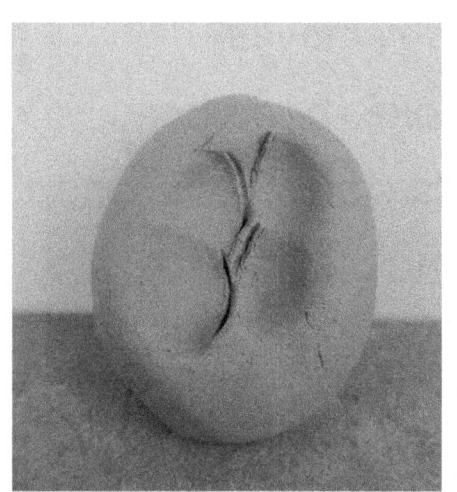

you may wish to model are either round or spherical. Most animal or human figures are oval or egg shaped.

In these cases the trick is to start off by preparing the pieces roughly the same shape as the intended model, so to make a body the starting point would be to prepare an ovoid piece and make the thumb pot using this piece. You stand a much better chance of achieving your oval shape using this strategy. Using the prepared egg shape the first thing to do is to open up the clay as shown in the picture, hold the egg shape along the fingertips of both hands with the thumbs, knuckles together, on top of one end of the egg shape. Press the thumb tips into the clay forming two indentations, move the thumb tips along the egg shape and press them into the clay again. Repeat this along the length of the piece. The result should be as shown in the picture. The longer models will call for more indentations. In this case I found that with the weight of clay chosen four indentations were sufficient.

Check the overall shape against the template and begin to open the hollow to complete the shape.

Use your thumbs and fingers inside and outside the walls of the pot and gently press and squeeze the clay to stretch and extend it to the required thickness and overall oval shape.

Regularly check the thickness of the wall, the shape and size to make the model to the correct scale. It is necessary to keep the edges of the pot reasonably thick to enable the 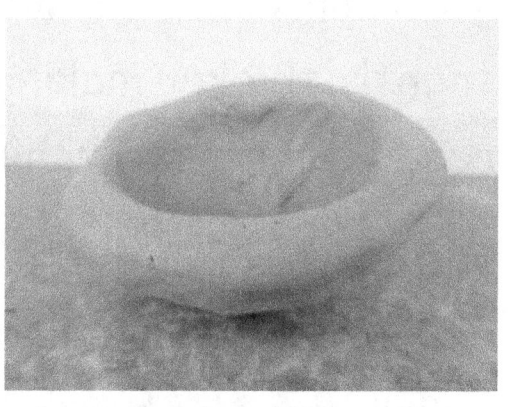 edge to support the weight of the body of the pot. Repeat the squeezing process until you are satisfied that you have matched the shape with the template.

Finally complete this part of the modelling by smoothing the surface of the pot with your fingers.

Make a second thumb pot.

Repeat the previous section to make a second, identical thumb pot, be sure that you follow the same process so that you will get the same result.

The next activity is to join the two pots along the rims, hold the two pots edge to edge to check that the diameters match and that there is sufficient clay to form a good seal at the joint.

Join two thumb pots.

One tip before we start the joining process, to give a better chance of matching the edges, hold each pot in your cupped hand and gently tap the edge on the work surface. This makes the edge level, smooth and slightly thicker making a level substantial surface ready for crosshatching.

With the point of the knife **crosshatch** both of the edges to be joined and create **slip** on both surfaces by rubbing the brush loaded with water across the crosshatch marks.

Hold one half of the body in the palm of your hand to support the edges and by holding the knife like a pencil you can use the sharp

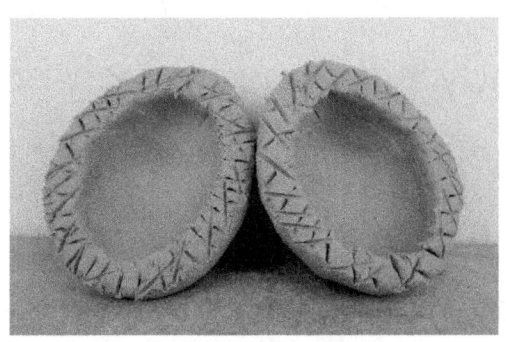

edge to score marks in the clay. Cut the marks into the surface in one direction, turning the clay around until the marks are completely round the edge. Reverse this process to make crosses on the whole surface as shown on the picture.

Repeat this process on the other half of the head before applying slip.

*The creation of **slip** is an important part of joining together two pieces of clay. The water from the brush is rubbed firmly into the clay surface until it turns light grey*

*Crosshatching** is one of the keys to joining two pieces of clay. It consists of the scoring the pieces in the areas to be joined. Use the point of the knife to mark clay.*

*The use of **pressure** is essential in successfully joining two pieces of clay when used in conjunction with crosshatching and slip.*

Creating slip on the crosshatch marks in this manner allows water to penetrate the crosshatch marks into the clay surface forming a larger surface area for the water to soften and help to form the slip.

When you have prepared slip on both halves of the body hold one in each hand, bring the two prepared surfaces into contact and press them firmly together with a slight sliding motion across the surfaces to ensure that you get a good bond. The next part

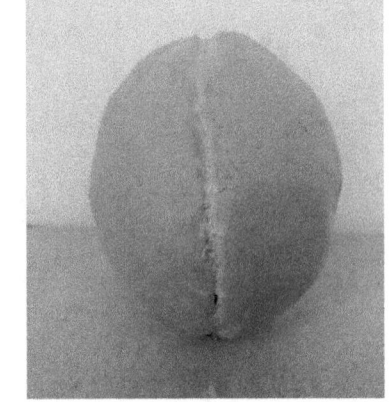

of the process is to seal and hide the joint. First, with the tip of your thumb or finger scrape clay from one half of the head to the other alternating the strokes, one way then the other to give an even distribution. Use the flat surface of the knife blade like a spatula to further smooth and tidy the join.

At this stage the body is an egg shaped piece of clay again, in fact it is actually a bubble of air surrounded by clay.

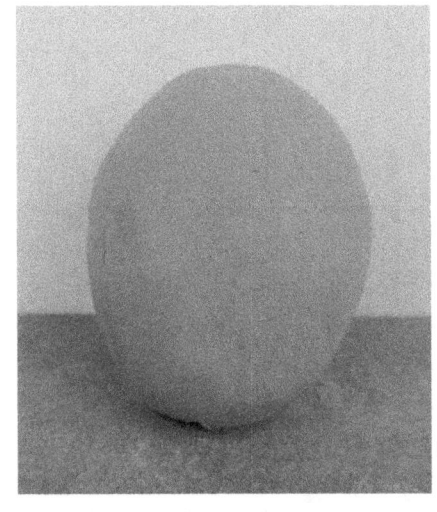

Finally take the hollow piece of clay in the palms of your hands and treat it like a solid piece by rolling it between your palms as you did in preparation, rolling it until it is smooth and free from blemishes. Final smoothing of the bubble of clay can be done on a plastic work surface if a really smooth surface is required.

Make the shoulders.

The shoulders are again a single oval thumb pot, but more elongated than the ones made for the head.

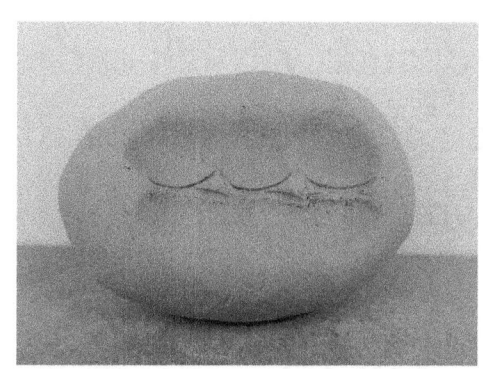 Start by rolling the clay into a smooth ball and then into a short sausage shape, round off the ends of the sausage shape, modelling the ends with pressure from your thumbs and fingers. Hold the clay between fingers of both hands place both thumbs together at one end of the sausage shape with nails and knuckles touching.

Press your joined thumbs into the clay making a double hole with the thumbs. Move your joined thumbs a little further along the sausage shape and make two more holes, repeat this until you are almost at the end of the clay which now has a series of holes ready to make a complete thumb pot.

Check the overall shape against the template and begin to open the hollow to complete the shape.

Use your thumbs and fingers inside and outside the walls of the pot and gently press and squeeze the clay to stretch and extend it to the required thickness and overall oval shape.

The shape is designed to be reasonably thick and sturdy as it has to support the combined weight of the head, features and kneck when it is complete.

Make and fit the neck.

The neck takes the form of a thick disk.

Roll the clay into a smooth ball, squash it partially flat using the template for guidance to size and shape.

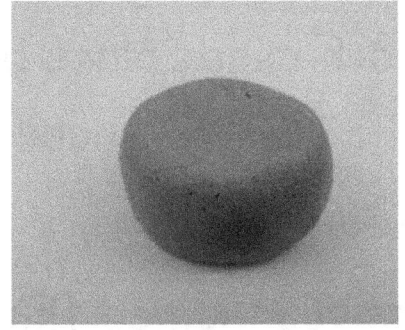

Having flattened the ball into a disc you can then roll the disc on the edge to make it less rounded.

Complete the shaping using pressure from your fingers and thumbs.

Crosshatch one side of the disc and a patch the same size at the centre of the shoulders. Create slip on both the head and the shoulders and press the neck firmly onto the shoulders, remember to support the inside of the shoulders with one hand while pressing the neck onto the top.

Fitting the head to the shoulders is the next task

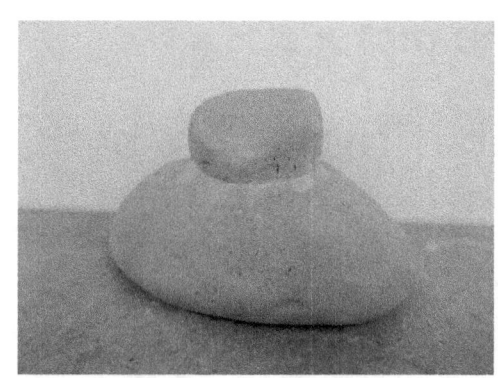 and starts by forming a groove in the neck in which the head will be supported and tilted to resemble a human head with a protruding chin.

Create the groove with your thumb while supporting the head and shoulders between fingers and thumb of the other hand.

Balance the head in the groove with the chin protruding and when you are satisfied with the position of the head mark the position on the head with the pointed stick by carefully drawing a line where the neck touches the head.

When you have marked the head and before we fix it in position it is a convenient point to press clay from the neck onto the shoulders and to form the shape of the neck by blending and smoothing the joint with finger and thumbs.

This makes it more realistic and actually strengthens the joint.

Crosshatch the area within the groove and inside the mark on the head as shown in the picture.

With water on the slip brush rub it firmly into both crosshatched areas to make slip.

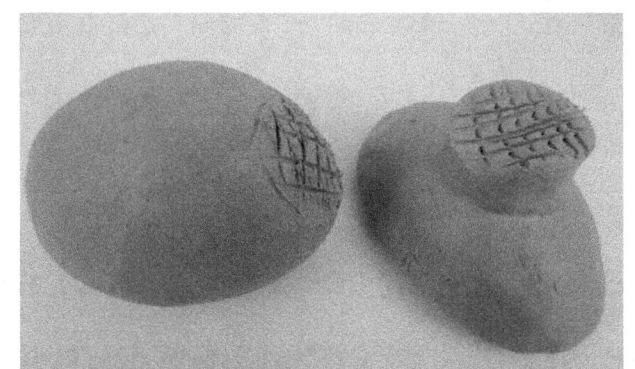

While fitting the head onto the neck and shoulders support the neck using your fingers inside the shoulders, this will ensure that you don't push the neck into the shoulders.

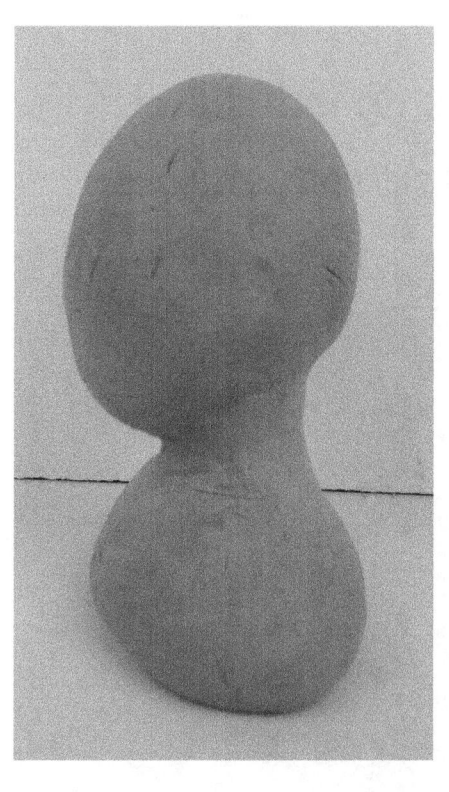

Press the two areas of slip firmly together with sufficient pressure to form a good bond between the two pieces of clay.

When the head is fixed in place you can mould the clay from neck into the clay on the head.

Use your thumbs or fingers to blend the clay and hide the joint.

Finish off the smoothing and moulding using the smooth edge of the plastic knife like a spatula. Once again the blending of the clay around a joint helps to strengthen the joint by effectively forming a single piece of clay rather than two joined pieces.

Decorate and detail the model.

This is where your model becomes an individual creation I will describe what I used to make the model that you see, you can copy the model or use and develop the techniques to design your own version. Just remember to be careful not to squash the head, support it when you are working on it and always use slip and pressure to stick the pieces together.

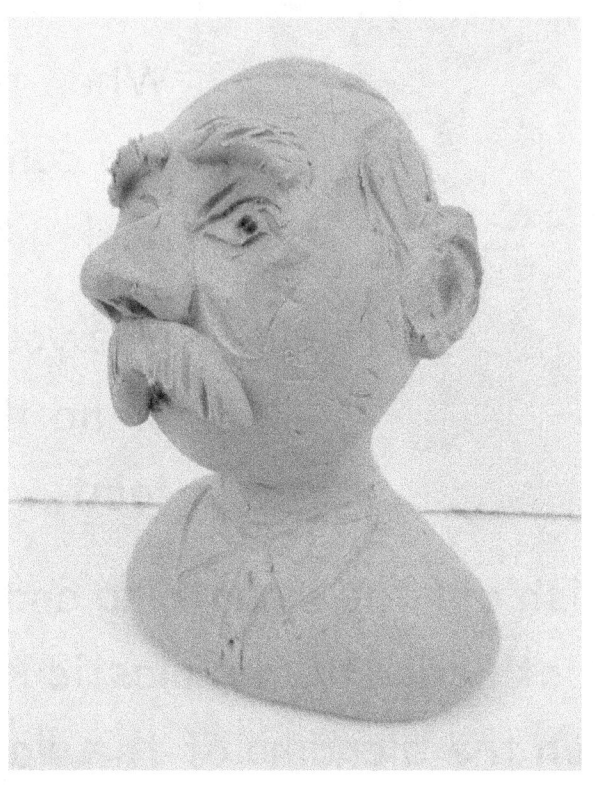

Start with the eyes, place them in the centre of the face, as your eyes are generally set into the face make two indentations with finger or thumb.

Also make two shallow indentations or hollows near the eyes to form the temples.

The nose starts off as a ball which is pressed onto the work surface pinched between thumb and finger

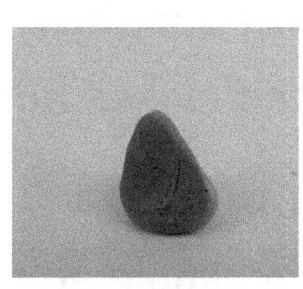 to form the sharp edge of the nose. Press the clay with your thumb to form the end of the nose and to push out the nostrils.

The moustache and eyebrows were all started as sausage shapes pointed at both ends as shown on the picture. Eyebrows are bent to follow the eye socket and fixed into position with slip. Flatten and smooth them to suit your design using the sharp edge of the knife to draw lines detailing hair.

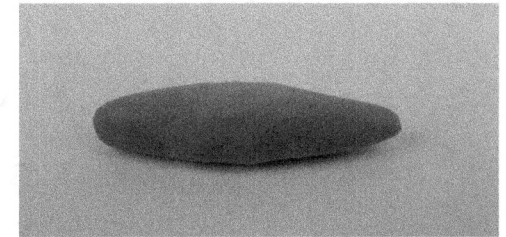

The moustache was bent like a banana, flattened and slipped into place. The knife point or edge was used to create the hair.

Ears started as a ball shape which was squashed in the palm of the hand to form a disc and cut in half.

Create slip on the head and on the back of the ear which is formed and then pressed onto the head level with the top of the eyes.

Using the pointed stick or a sharp pencil detail the ears, eyes and hair using a friend as a model.

In my model the mouth is virtually hidden but the pointed stick pushed under his moustache makes him sing or whistle.

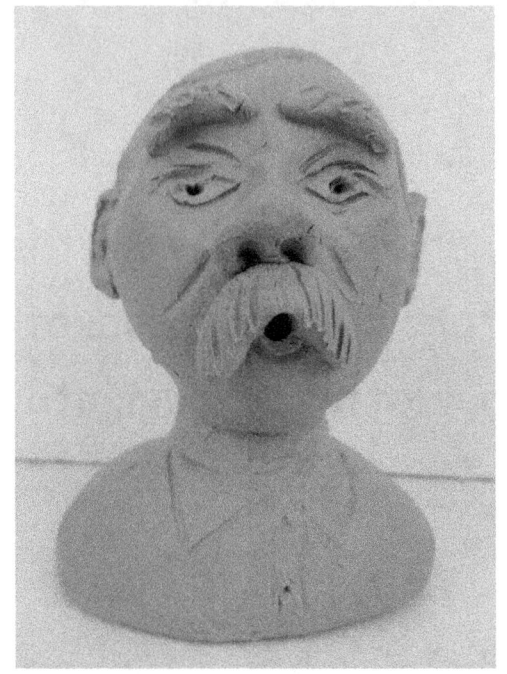

Finally I added a simple shirt collar to decorate the shoulders.

You now know how to create a basic head shape and with a bit of creative thought you could create a model of anyone's head.

Enjoy your clay modelling.

Brian.

B & M Potterycrafts.

Double Thumb Pot. Head and Shoulders.

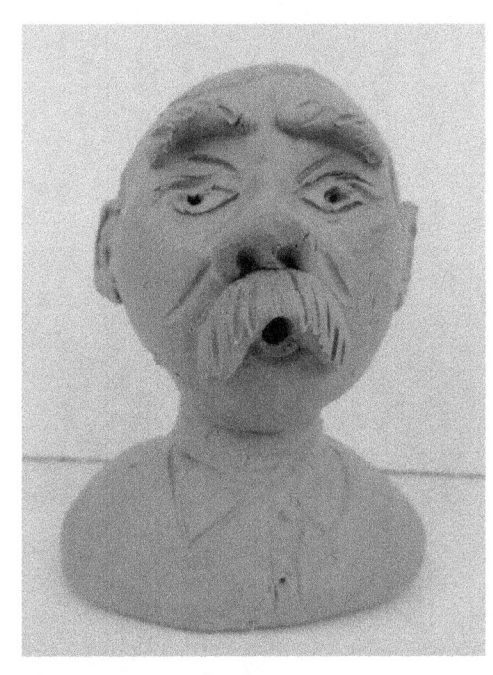

Clay.

Head. 80 gramsx2.

Neck. 20 grams.

Shoulders. 120 grams.

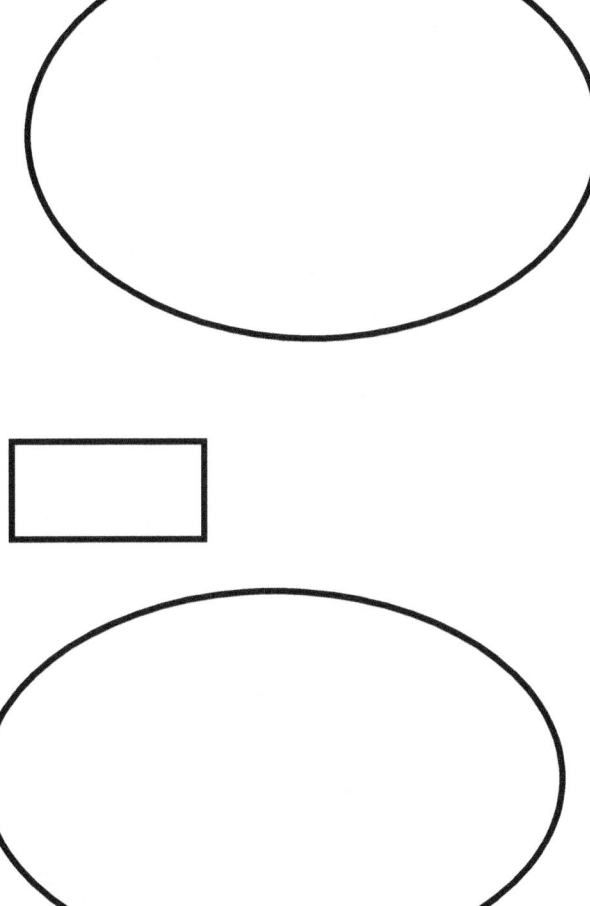

40

B & M Potterycrafts.

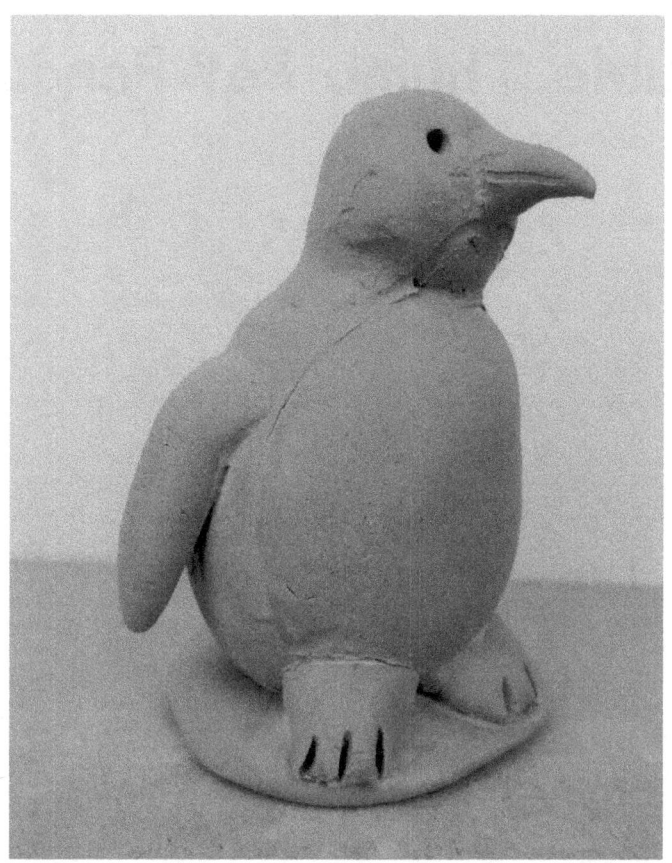

Clay modelling projects.

Double Thumb Pot Penguin.

Create the model shown on this cover by following step by step, easy to understand, instructions supported by still photos at each stage.

Brian Rollins.

B & M Potterycrafts.

Double Thumb Pot Penguin.

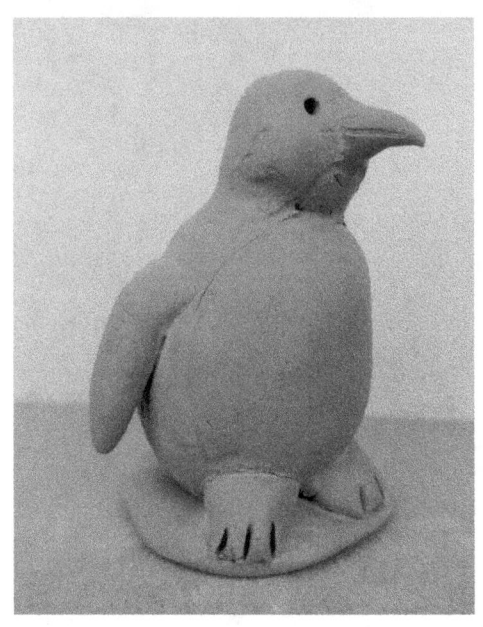

Contents and sequence.

Make the body.

Make and fit the head.

Make and fit the feet and tail.

Make and fit the wings.

Make and fit the beak.

Decorate and detail the model.

Penguin worksheet.

Double Thumb Pot Penguin.

Make the body.

Roll a ball.

Roll the clay between the palms of your hands, exerting sufficient force to remove any lumps or

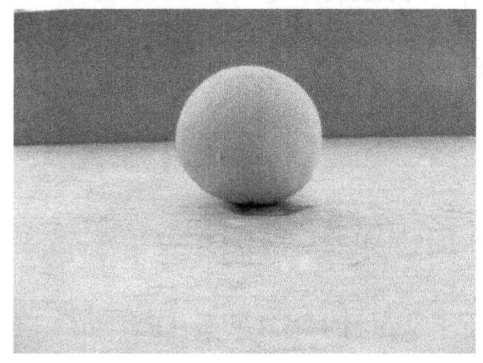

bumps. Don't be tempted to take the easy route to smooth the clay by rolling it on the wooden work surface as this removes moisture from the clay and could

make it too hard for modelling. Any creases or cracks can be smoothed using the fingers. Continue to roll the clay until the surface is smooth and the clay is the desired shape ie a ball shape.

Make an egg shape.

Take the clay ball between the palms of your hands and roll it into an egg shape. Roll the clay backwards and forwards across your palms exerting sufficient pressure to form the egg shape. The

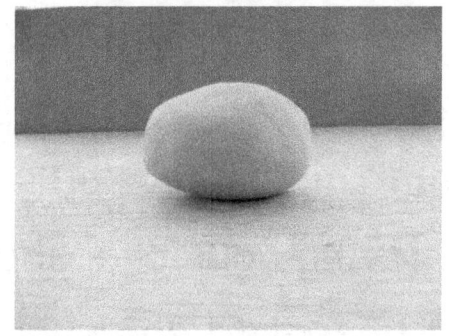

best way is to roll the clay a few times, check the

shape then roll it a bit more, keep rolling and checking until you get the shape that you need. Complete the shape by rounding off the ends of the egg with your fingers.

Prepare an oval (irregular) thumb pot.

By irregular thumb pots I mean any thumb pot which does not start with a sphere of clay or does not finish as a spherical shape.

The requirement for an oval shape rather than a round or spherical one is that very few figures which you may wish to model are either round or spherical. Most animal or human figures are oval or egg shaped.

In these cases the trick is to start off by preparing 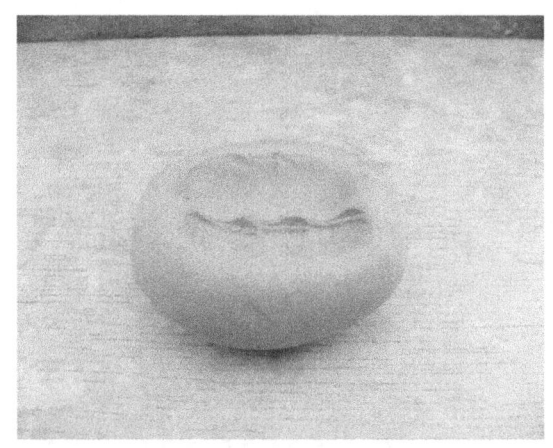 the pieces roughly the same shape as the intended model, so to make a body the starting point would be to prepare an ovoid piece and make the thumb pot from this piece. You stand a much better chance of achieving your oval shape using this strategy. Using the prepared egg shape the first thing to do is to open up the clay as shown in the picture, hold the egg shape along the finger tips of both hands with the thumbs, knuckles together on top of one end of the egg shape. Press the thumb tips into the clay forming two indentations, move the thumb tips along the egg shape and press them into the clay again. Repeat this along the length of the piece. The result should be as shown in the picture. The longer models will call for more indentations.

Check the overall shape against the template and begin to open the hollow to complete the shape.

Use your thumbs and fingers inside and outside the walls of the pot and gently press and squeeze the clay to stretch and extend it to the required thickness and overall oval shape.

Regularly check the thickness of the wall, the shape and size to make the model to the correct scale. It is necessary to keep the

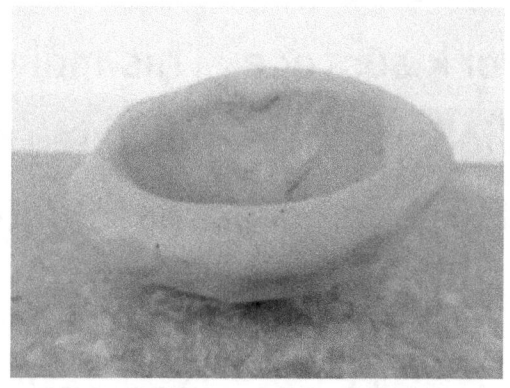

edges of the pot reasonably thick to enable the edge to support the weight of the body of the pot. Repeat the squeezing process until you are satisfied that you have matched the shape with the template.

Finally complete this part of the modelling by smoothing the surface of the pot with your fingers.

Make a second thumb pot.

Repeat the previous section to make a second, identical thumb pot, be sure that you follow the same process so that you will get the same result.

The next activity is to join the two pots along the rims, hold the two pots edge to edge to check that the diameters match and that there is sufficient clay to form a good seal at the joint.

Join two thumb pots.

One tip before we start the joining process, to give a better chance of matching the edges, hold each pot in your cupped hand and gently tap the edge on the work surface. This makes the edge level, smooth and slightly thicker making a level substantial surface ready for crosshatching.

With the point of the knife **crosshatch** both of the edges to be joined and create **slip** on both surfaces by rubbing the brush loaded with water across the crosshatch marks.

Hold one half of the body in the palm of your hand to support the edges and by holding the knife like a 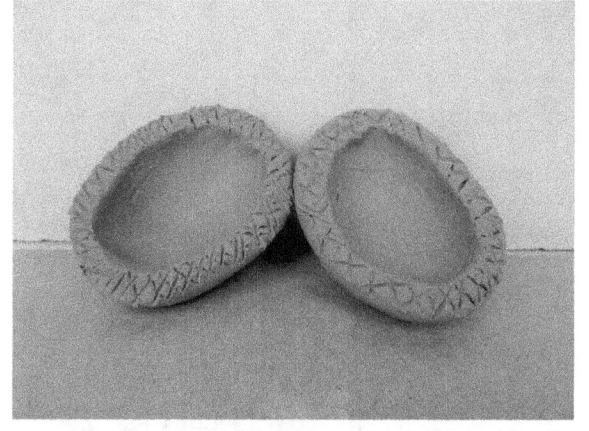 pencil you can use the sharp edge to score marks in the clay. Cut the marks into the surface in one direction, turning the half body around until the marks are round the complete shape. Reverse this process to make crosses on the whole surface as shown on the picture.

Repeat this process on the other half of the body before applying slip.

*The creation of **slip** is an important part of joining together two pieces of clay. The water from the brush is rubbed firmly into the clay surface until it turns light grey*

***Crosshatching** is one of the keys to joining two pieces of clay. It consists of the scoring the pieces in the areas to be joined. Use the point of the knife to mark clay.*

*The use of **pressure** is essential in successfully joining two pieces of clay when used in conjunction with crosshatching and slip.*

Creating slip on the crosshatch marks in this manner allows water to penetrate the crosshatch marks into the clay surface forming a larger surface area for the water to soften and help to form the slip.

When you have prepared slip on both halves of the body hold one in each hand, bring the two prepared surfaces into contact and press them firmly together with a slight sliding motion across the surfaces to ensure that you get a good bond. The next part of the

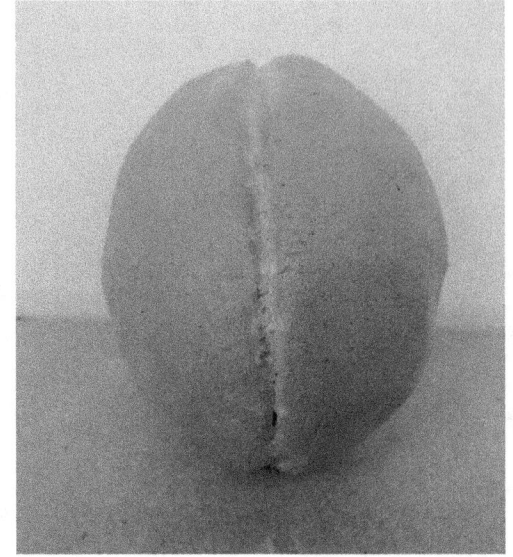

process is to seal and hide the joint. First, with the tip of your thumb or finger scrape clay from one half of the body to the other alternating the strokes, one way then the other to give an even distribution. Use the flat surface of the knife blade like a spatula to further smooth and tidy the join.

At this stage the body is an egg shaped piece of clay

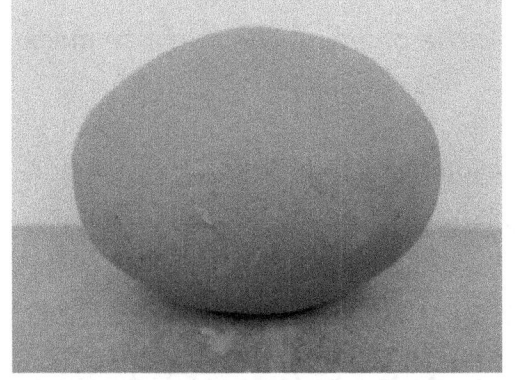

again, in fact it is actually a bubble of air surrounded by clay.

Finally take the hollow piece of clay in the palms of your hands and treat it like a solid piece by rolling it between your palms as you did in preparation, rolling it until it is smooth and free from blemishes. Final smoothing of the bubble of clay can be done on a plastic work surface if a really smooth surface is required.

Head to body.

Start by rolling the clay into a smooth ball and stand the body on one end .To attach the head to the body we need to make **crosshatch** marks and create **slip.** With the point of the plastic knife score '**#**' on the

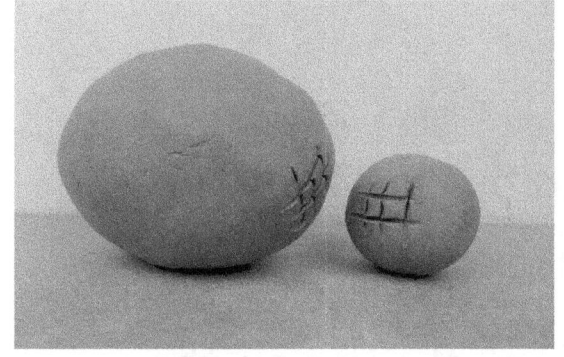

top of the body and on the head where it is to be joined to the body. Dip the brush in water and firmly rub the brush and water across the '#' marks, the area will turn a lighter shade of grey, this material is **slip.** Finally **press** the head and body firmly together.

The creation of **slip** *is an important part of joining together two pieces of clay. The water from the brush is rubbed firmly into the clay surface until it turns light grey*

Crosshatching *is one of the keys to joining two pieces of clay. It consists of the scoring the pieces in the areas to be joined. Use the point of the knife to mark clay.*

*The use of **pressure** is essential in successfully joining two pieces of clay when used in conjunction with crosshatching and slip.*

After the head has been joined to the body the next step is to blend clay from the head into the body forming the neck and shoulders.

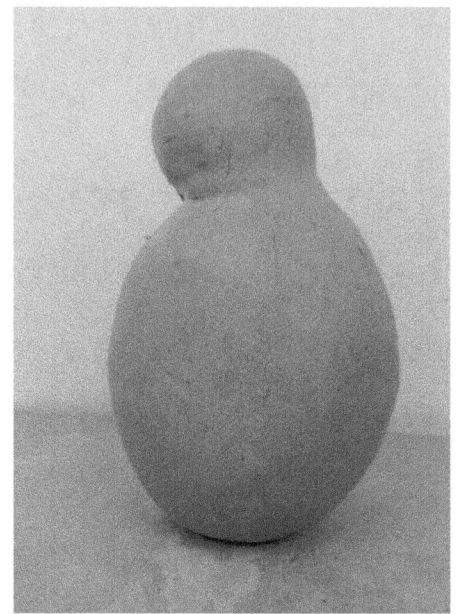

Hold the model upright in one hand and use the tip of your finger or thumb of the other hand to press clay from the head to the body.

Do this most of the way round but leave the area where the face will be, the front of the head.

When you have moved sufficient clay finish the activity by smoothing the joint with your fingers.

Make and fit the feet and tail.

First roll the clay into a smooth ball and then roll the

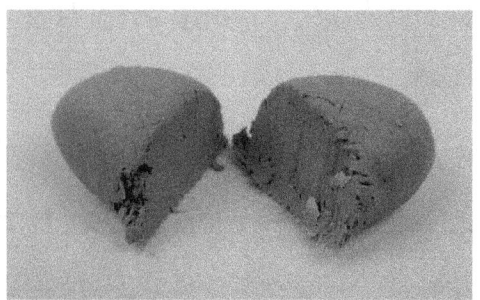

ball across the palms of your hands with slight pressure applied to form a short sausage shape cut this in half to make the feet. Mark the sausage shape across the centre then cut it in half when you are satisfied that the mark is in the middle.

To make the tail the clay must first be rolled into a ball. Roll one edge of the ball across the palm of one hand using one finger this method of rolling will produce a short cone shape, when the cone is the required length flatten the thick end on the work surface.

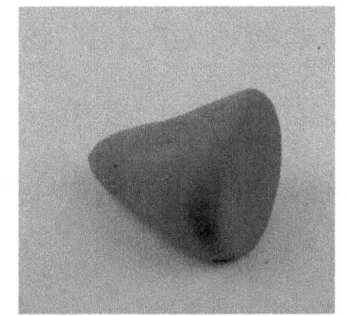

Use the brush and water to form slip in two patches where the feet are to fit, make slip on the feet where they have been cut and press the feet into place smoothing the joint underneath the body to strengthen it. Penguins have flat feet so after assembly slightly squash the feet and flatten them a little with your finger.

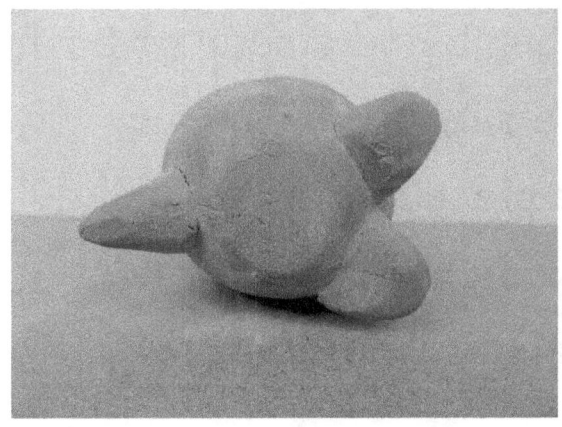

Create slip on the flattened end of the tail and also on the penguin where the tail will fit, press the tail firmly into place. When the tail is firmly in place press the penguin slightly forward against the feet to make it lean forwards a little.

Make and fit the wings.

Penguins' wings have more or less evolved into flippers and this is how they are used when the penguins are swimming, in fact they look as though they are flying under water. The wings are short and stiff so we need to make them quite thick.

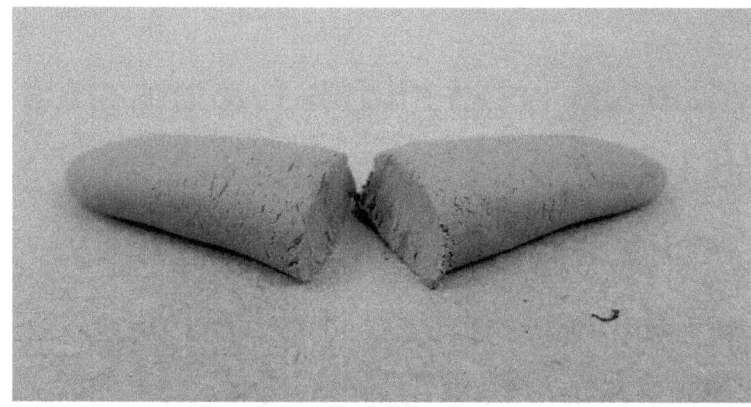 To start making the wing roll the clay into a ball then roll the ball into a sausage to the length shown on the worksheet. Form the ends of the sausage into a double cone shape by rolling the ends simultaneously between the thumb and finger of both hands. Squash the double cone slightly with your thumb then cut the flattened piece in half to make the wings Create slip on the body where the wings are to fit and on the wing where it will touch the body.

Press the wings firmly into place and smooth the tops to form them to the body.

Make and fit the beak.

Start the beak by rolling the clay into a ball and then into a cone shape between the index finger and thumb of the hand. And flatten the thick end on the work surface. Create slip at the front of the head and on

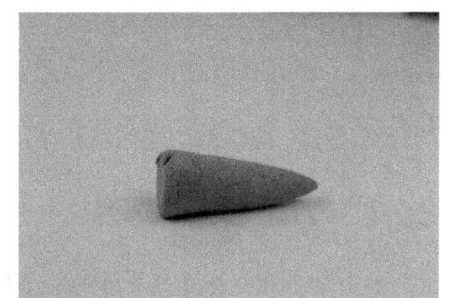

the thick end of the beak then press the beak into place.

Make the base and fit the penguin.

Prepare the clay by rolling it into a ball, then squash it as shown in the picture, roughly into the size and

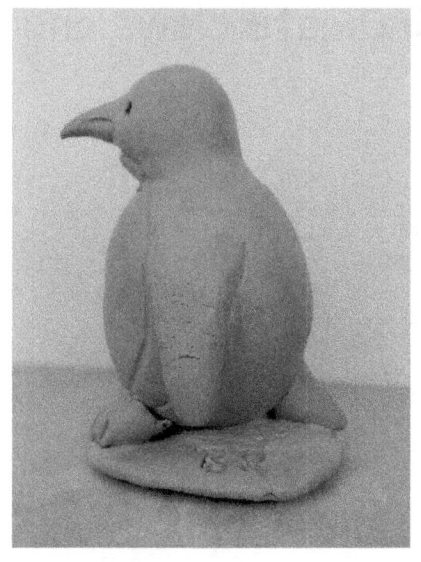

shape of the pancake shape which you need. Try to ensure that the thickness is the same across the whole surface of the slab. If it is too thick in places the figure attached will be sloping. If it is too thin in parts the piece will be weak.

Crosshatch the underside of the model and the base in the areas where the model will touch. Apply water with the brush to the model and the base creating slip on each piece. Finally press the model firmly down onto the base taking care not to distort the shape.

Please note *that if you intend to fire the model and to avoid damaging it make a small vent hole through the base and into the body to release steam.*

Apply details.
Use the point of the wooden stick to make two holes for the penguin's eyes.

Complete the decoration by drawing a line round the front of the penguin where his white shirt will show. Also use the point of the knife to indicate claws and the sides of the beak.

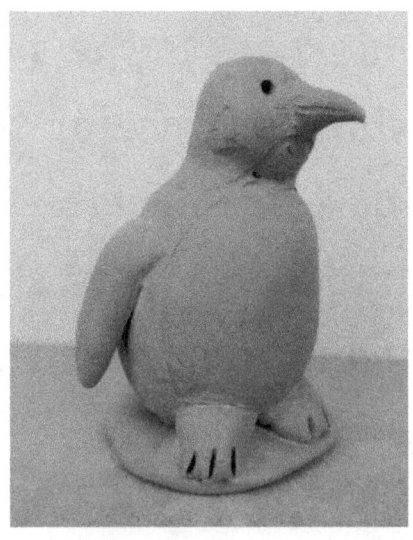

B & M Potterycrafts.

Penguin. Double thumb pot.

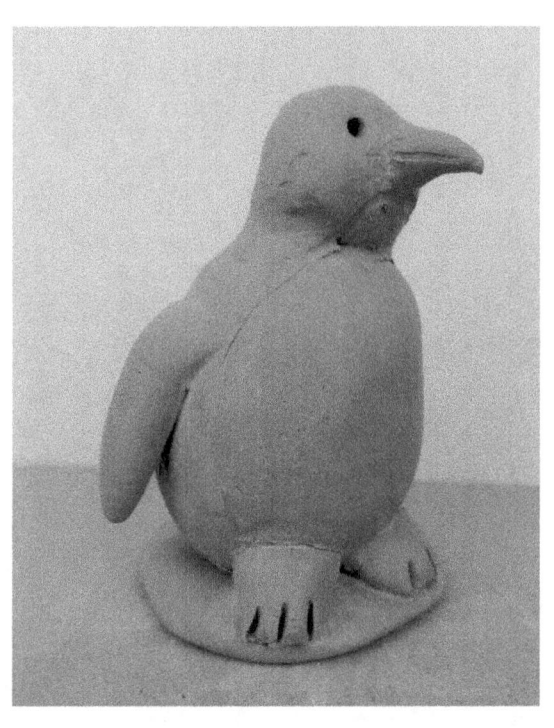

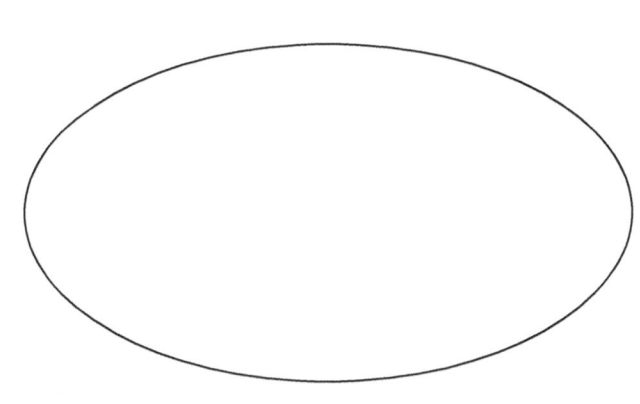

Body.   100+100 grams.

Head.   35 grams.

Feet.   10 grams.

Tail.   5 grams.

Beak.   1 gram.

Wings.   18 grams.

Base.   60 grams.

Scale.   [   ]   **5 cms.**

B & M Potterycrafts.

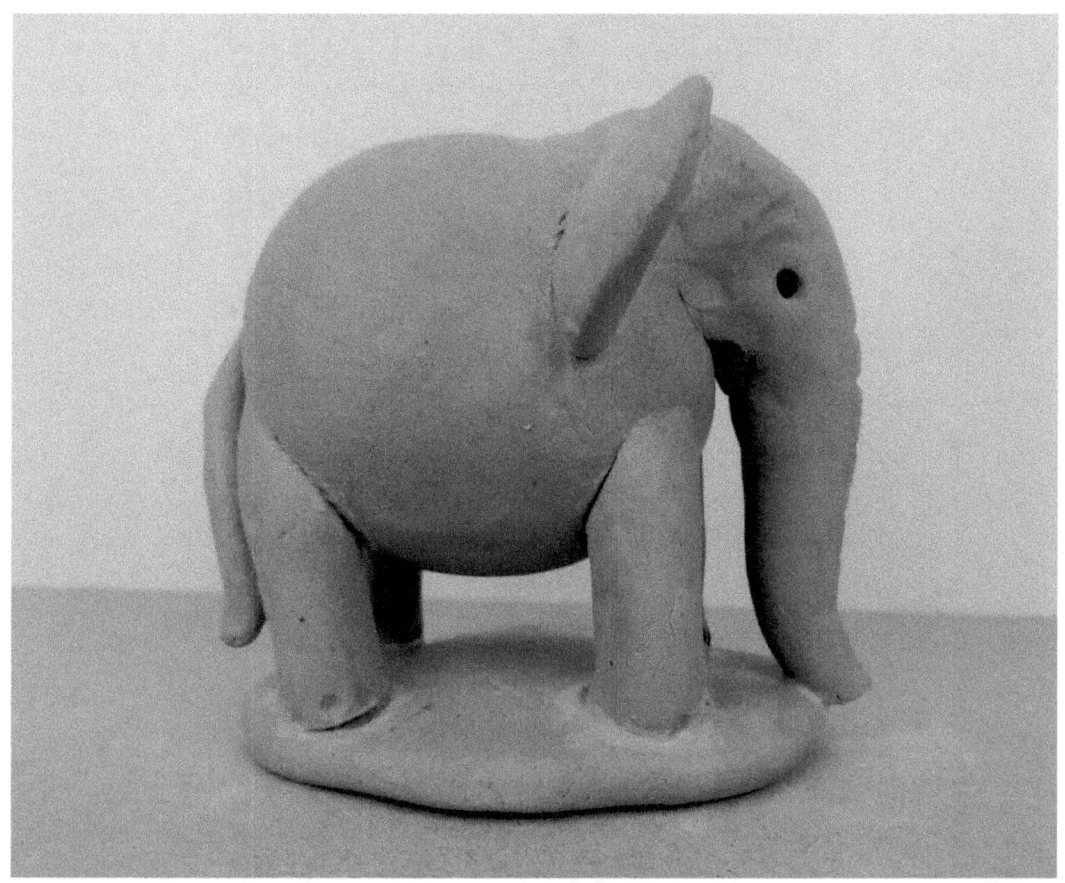

Clay modelling projects.

Double Thumb Pot Elephant.

Create the model shown on this cover by following step by step, easy to understand, instructions supported by still photos at each stage.

Brian Rollins.

B & M Potterycrafts.

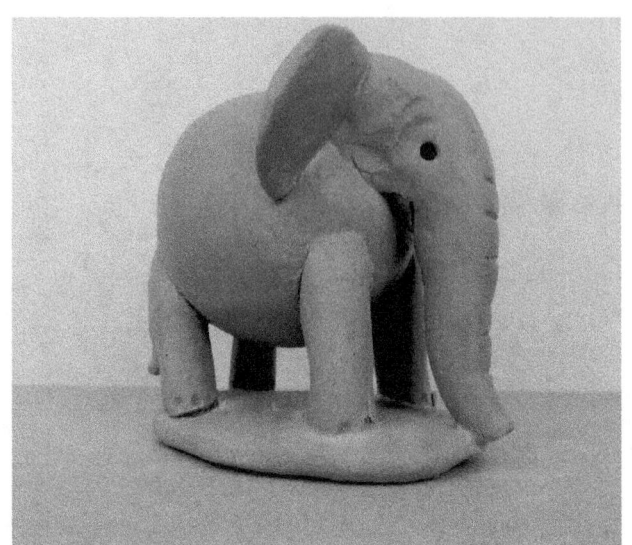

Double Thumb Pot Elephant.

Contents and sequence.

Roll a ball.

Create a single thumb pot.

Make a second thumb pot.

Join two thumb pots.

Make and fit the legs.

Make and fit the trunk.

Make and fit the ears.

Make and fit the tail.

Detail the face.

Make the base and fit the elephant.

Worksheet.

Double thumb pot elephant.

Create a single thumb pot.

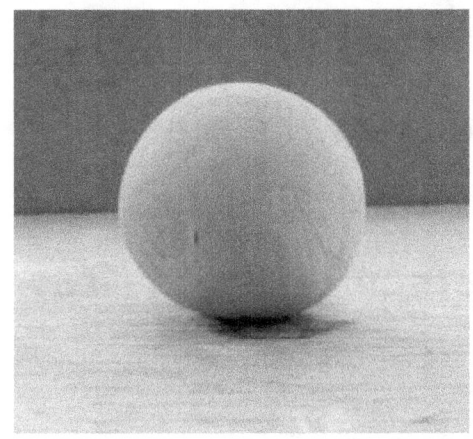

The first part in creating a thumb pot from a ball of clay is to ensure that the ball is round and smooth.

Roll the clay between the palms of your hands, exerting sufficient force to remove any lumps or bumps. Don't be tempted to take the easy route to smooth the clay by rolling it on the wooden work surface as this removes moisture from the clay and could make it too hard for modelling. Any creases or cracks can be smoothed using the fingers. Continue to roll the clay until the surface is smooth and the clay is the desired shape i.e. a ball shape.

The main reasons for this are that if the clay is not smooth before you start to stretch it any cracks will appear as a weakness and the clay will split at those points, to get round this problem check for cracks after each stage of the hollowing and stretching process, smooth out any cracks around the edge with pressure from your fingers.

Please note that if the clay isn't spherical before you start to form the pot you have little chance of finishing with a circular thumb pot.

To start the thumb pot hold the clay in the tips if the fingers of both hands with both thumbs touching the clay, put the thumb nails together until the first knuckles touch each other.
Now press your thumbs firmly into the clay leaving two clear impressions like the ones in the picture.

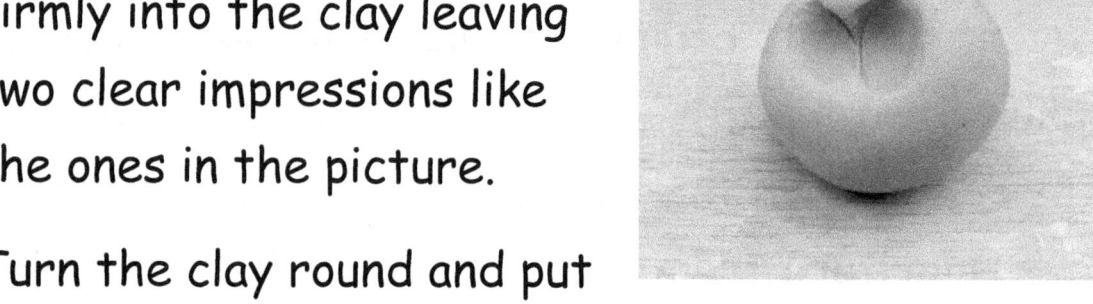

Turn the clay round and put your thumbs back into the hole and press your thumbs into the clay again, making the hole deeper. You can now use the pressure of your thumbs inside the pot against the fingers outside the pot to make the hole deeper and wider, turn the pot round as you gently squeeze the sides of the pot. At this point measure the diameter of your pot against the template on the worksheet, which is the diameter of the pot that you are aiming for. The overall effect can be likened to a half ball or the top of a mushroom.

Because we are making two thumb pots which have to

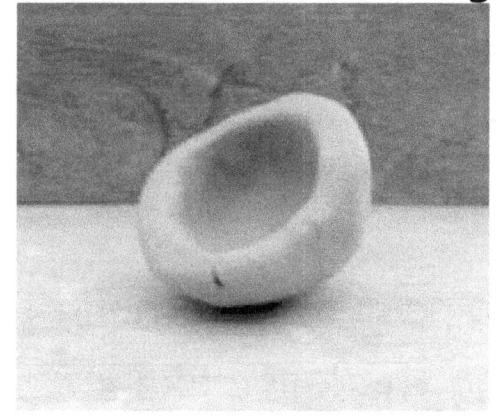

be joined along the rims these rims need to be thick enough to form a substantial joint. Make sure that the rims are not too thin and that the thickness of the pot sides is carried through to the edge.

Make a second thumb pot.

Repeat the previous section to make a second, identical thumb pot, be sure that you follow the same process so that you will get the same result.

The next activity is to join the two pots along the rims, hold the two pots edge to edge to check that the diameters match and that there is sufficient clay to form a good seal at the joint.

Join two thumb pots.

One tip before we start the joining process, to give a better chance of matching the edges, hold each pot in your cupped hand and gently tap the edge on the work surface. This makes the edge level, smooth and slightly thicker making a level substantial surface ready for crosshatching.

With the point of the knife **crosshatch** both of the edges to be joined and create **slip** on both surfaces by rubbing the brush loaded with water across the crosshatch marks.

Hold one half of the body in the palm of your hand to support the edges and by holding the knife like a

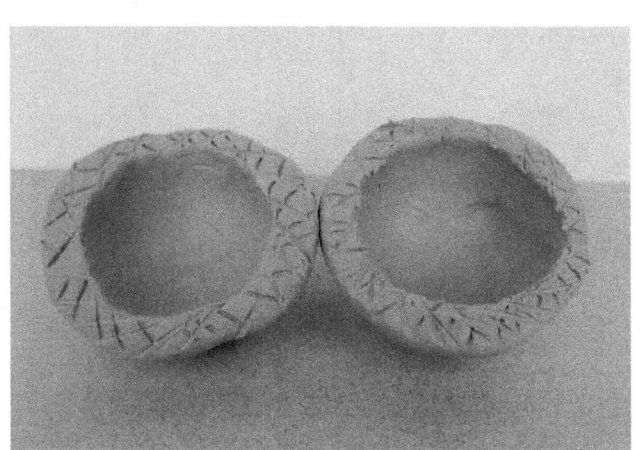

pencil you can use the sharp edge to score marks in the clay. Cut the marks into the surface in one direction, turning the half sphere around until the marks are round the complete circle. Reverse this process to make crosses on the whole surface as shown on the picture.

Repeat this process on the other half sphere before applying slip.

*The creation of **slip** is an important part of joining together two pieces of clay. The water from the brush is rubbed firmly into the clay surface until it turns light grey*

Crosshatching *is one of the keys to joining two pieces of clay. It consists of the scoring the pieces in the areas to be joined. Use the point of the knife to mark clay.*

*The use of **pressure** is essential in successfully joining two pieces of clay when used in conjunction with crosshatching and slip.*

Creating slip on the crosshatch marks in this manner allows water to penetrate the crosshatch marks into the clay surface forming a larger surface area for the water to soften and help to form the slip.

When you have prepared slip on both halves of the body hold one in each hand, bring the two prepared 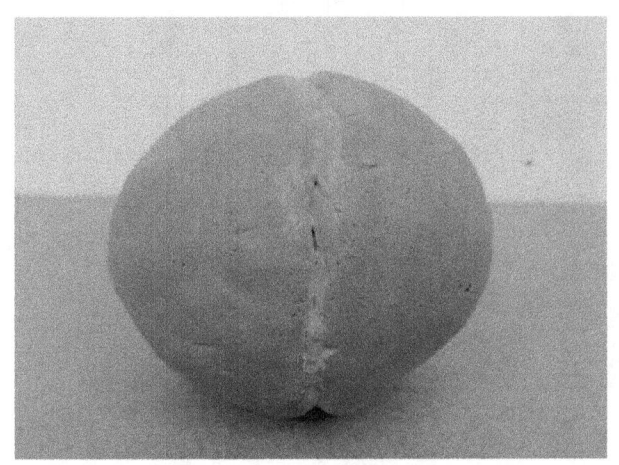 surfaces into contact and press them firmly together with a slight sliding motion across the surfaces to ensure that you get a good bond. The next part of the process is to seal and hide the joint. First, with the tip of your thumb or finger scrape clay from one half - sphere to the other alternating the strokes, one way then the other to give an even distribution. Use the flat surface of the knife blade like a spatula to further smooth and tidy the join.

At this stage the body is a ball shaped piece of clay again, in fact it is actually a bubble of air surrounded by clay.

Finally take the hollow ball of clay in the palms of your hands and treat it like a solid ball by rolling it between your palms as you did in preparation, rolling it until it is smooth and free from blemishes. Final smoothing of the bubble of clay can be done on a plastic work surface if a really smooth surface is required.

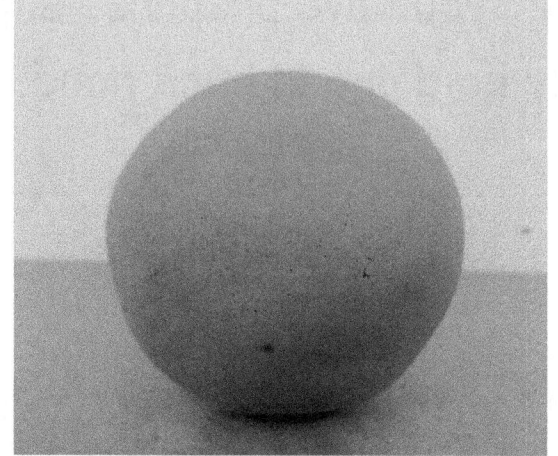

Make and fit the legs.
We make the legs two at a time in the following manner.

Take the clay in the palms of your hands and roll it onto a sausage shape, try to maintain a uniform thickness along the length of the sausage shape. Check the length against the template and finally

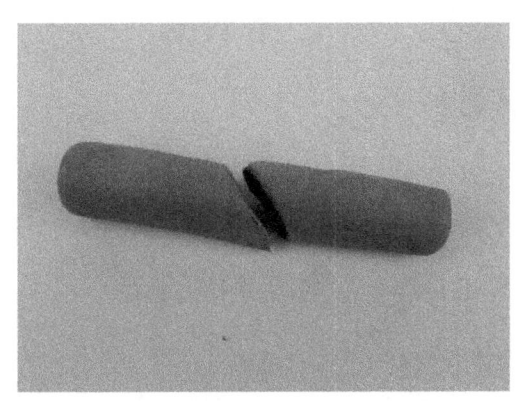

tidy up the ends by tapping the sausage shape on the work surface.

In this model we are making the legs in two pairs for the front and the back because the legs will be fitted in a manner to allow us to position them as far forward and backwards as possible. To achieve this we cut the sausage shape in half across a diagonal line which means that the legs can be positioned on the curve of the body, partly underneath the body and partly on front or side.

Check the first picture showing the legs in position to see what I mean.

Mark the clay across the centre with a diagonal mark in order to make both legs the same length, cut the clay cleanly once you are satisfied that the mark is in the centre. Reshape the legs into cylindrical forms and crosshatch the diagonal end of each leg as shown in the next picture.

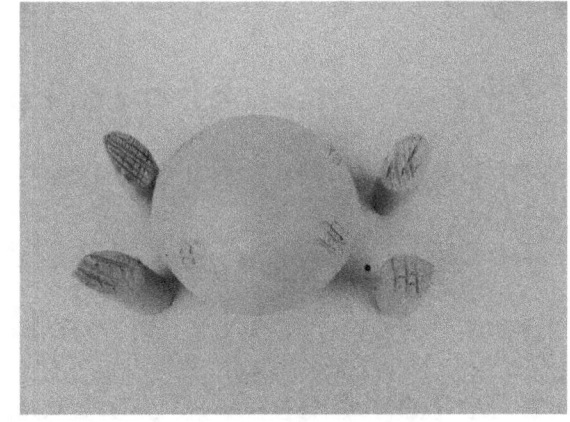

Having completed the first two legs repeat the process and make the other pair of legs.

Crosshatch the front and underside of the elephant's body in the areas where the legs are to be fitted. The positioning is shown on the picture.

Create slip on the body and on each leg by rubbing water into the crosshatch marks with the brush.

In order to prevent distortion in the ball of clay

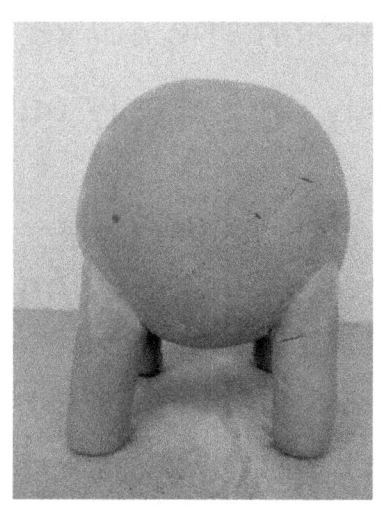

support the body in the palm of one hand while you press and twist the legs into poition.

With four legs firmly in place stand the model on the legs while you adjust the position of the legs if necessary.

Make and fit the trunk.

The creation of a carrot/cone shape for the trunk involves a special rolling skill. Instead of laying the hand flat on the clay as if to roll a sausage shape the hand is placed at an angle trapping the

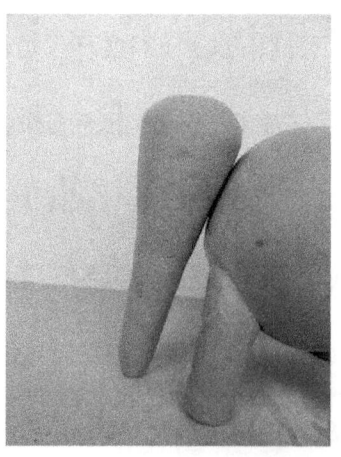

piece of clay you wish to extend between the hand and the work surface. With sufficient pressure to reform the clay using long rolls across the work surface until the carrot is the form and length required.

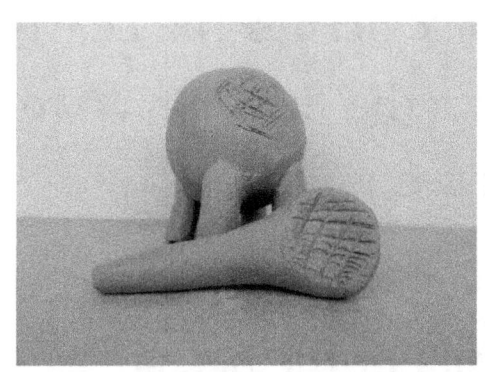

To complete the trunk shape you take the thick end of the carrot shape between the thumb and the first two fingers and squash it to form a spoon shape and place it in position at the front of the head.

To fit the trunk to the body crosshatch the inside surface of the spoon and the front of the head, create slip in these areas and press the trunk onto the front of the head.

Complete the fitting of the trunk by drawing the clay from the trunk onto the head all around the spoon shape with the fingers smoothing and hiding the joint as shown in the picture.

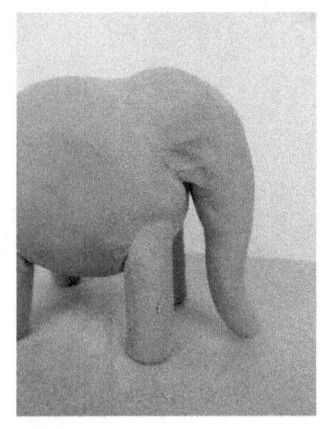

Make and fit the ears.

The ears are started by rolling the clay into a smooth ball and squashing the ball between the palms of your

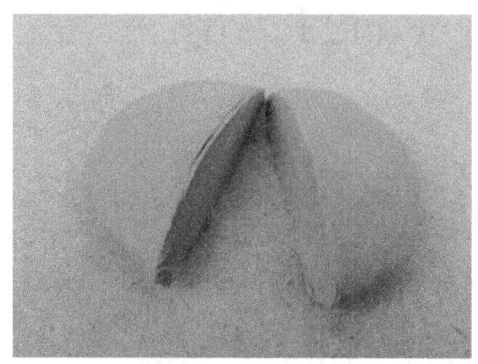

hands until you form a disc the same diameter as the template.

Mark the disc across the centre and then cut the disc in half to make two ears.

The ears are fitted to the back and side of the head as shown in the picture. Create slip in the areas where the ears are to be attached and in order to make the joint stronger the lower end of the ears are fixed to the elephant's back as well as to the head. Finally press the ears firmly into place.

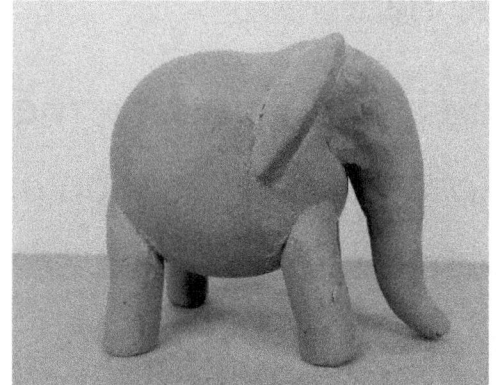

Make and fit the tail.

Roll the clay ito a short, thin sausage shape to form the tail, create a patch of slip on the spot where the tail is to attach and also along the length of the tail. To make a stronger , more substantial connection

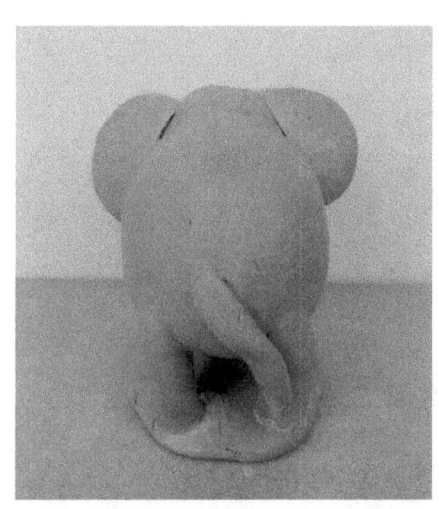

make slip down the back of one leg which gives a double point of connection.

Press one end of the tail into the body form a bend to line up with the leg and press the other end of the tail into position.

Make the base and fit the elephant.

Prepare the clay by rolling it into a ball, then squash it as shown in the picture, roughly into the size and shape of the pancake shape which you need. Try to ensure that the thickness is the same across the whole surface of the slab. If it is too thick in places the figure when it is attached it will be sloping. If it is too thin in parts the piece will be weak.

Mark the base where the feet touch and make crosshatch areas in these positions.

Crosshatch the ends of the legs and make slip on the base and on the legs. Place the ends of the legs onto the base and taking leg by leg press each one in turn onto the base.

Decorate the elephant.

If you are not sure where to position the details such as eyes you can refer to the picture in this section.

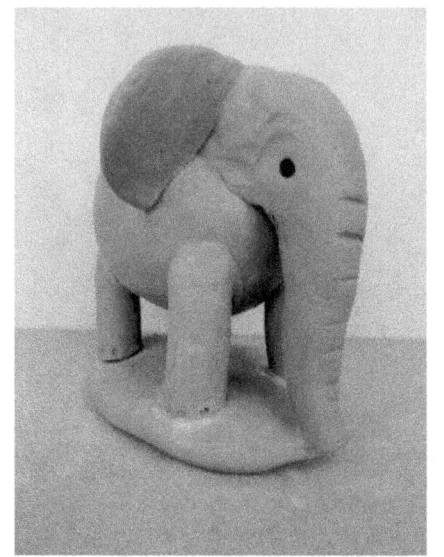

Complete the elephant using the pointed stick to make eyes and nostrils, simply push the pointed end of the stick into the clay to make the marks.

Use the rounded end of the stick for toenails pressing the edge five times into the top edge of each foot.

  Use and the edge of the knife for the wrinkles down the trunk pressing it into the clay to make the marks.

B. & M. Potterycrafts.

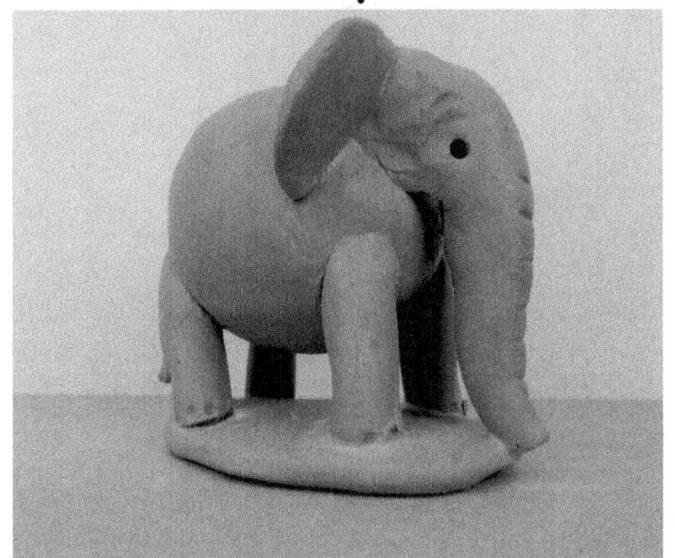

Inner Circle Ears. 4 cms.

Outer circle Body

6.5 cms.

Thumb Pot Elephant.

Clay.

Legs. 25grams. X2.

Trunk.   60 grams.

Ears.   20 grams.

Body.   100 grams × 2.

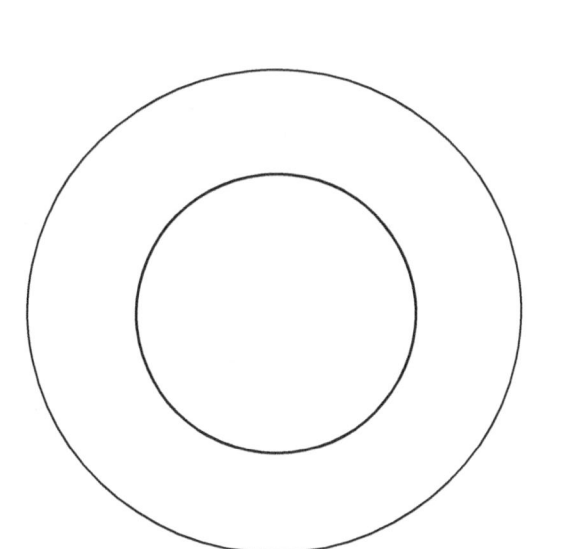

B & M Potterycrafts.

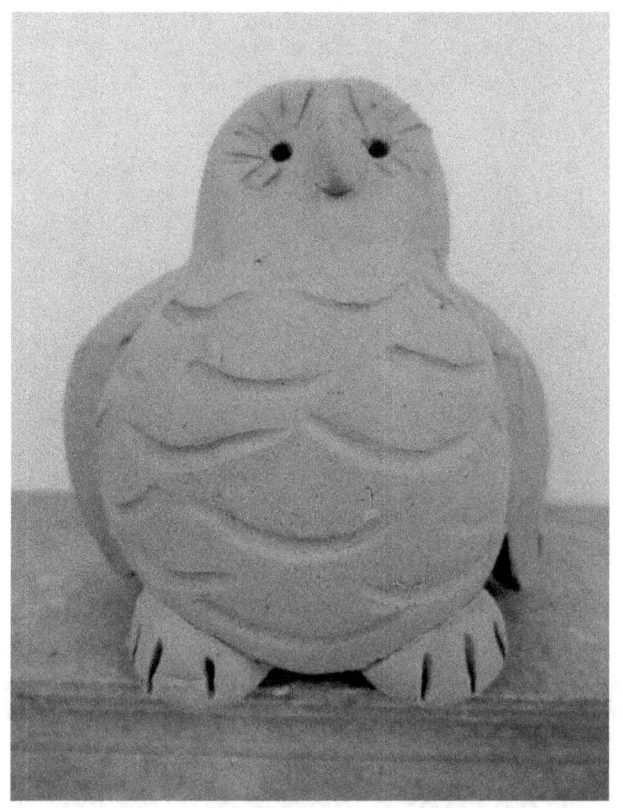

Clay modelling projects.

Double Thumb Pot Owl.

Olly.

Create the model shown on this cover by following step by step, easy to understand, instructions supported by still photos at each stage.

Brian Rollins.

B & M Potterycrafts.

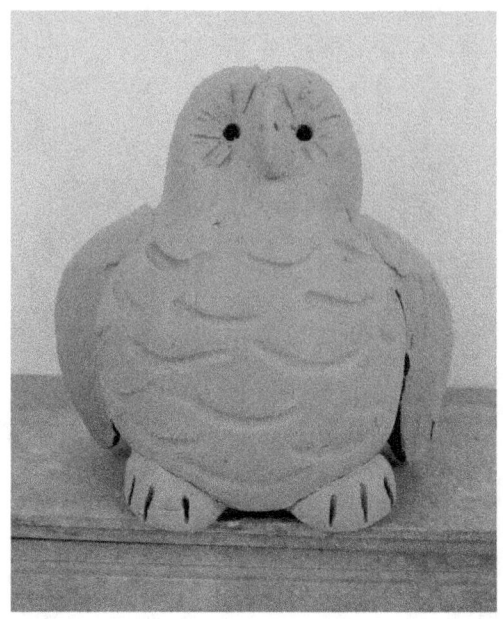

Double Thumb Pot Owl.

Contents and sequence.

Create a single thumb pot.

Make a second thumb pot.

Join two thumb pots.

Make and fit the head.

Make and fit the feet.

Make and fit the tail.

Make and fit the wings.

Decorate the model.

Worksheet.

Double thumb pot owl.

Create a single thumb pot.

The first part in creating a thumb pot from a ball of clay is to ensure that the ball is round and smooth.

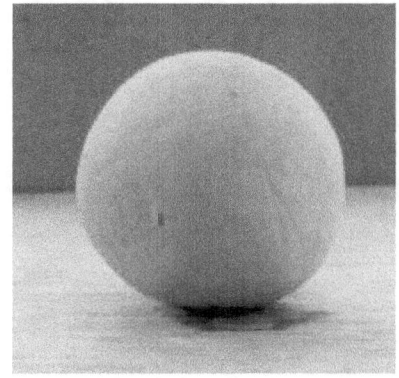 Roll the clay between the palms of your hands, exerting sufficient force to remove any lumps or bumps. Don't be tempted to take the easy route to smooth the clay by rolling it on the wooden work surface as this removes moisture from the clay and could make it too hard for modelling. Any creases or cracks can be smoothed using the fingers. Continue to roll the clay until the surface is smooth and the clay is the desired shape i.e. a ball shape.

The main reasons for this are that if the clay is not smooth before you start to stretch it any cracks will appear as a weakness and the clay will split at those points, to get round this problem check for cracks after each stage of the hollowing and stretching process, smooth out any cracks around the edge with pressure from your fingers.

Please note that if the clay isn't spherical before you start to form the pot you have little chance of finishing with a circular thumb pot.

To start the thumb pot hold the clay in the tips if the fingers of both hands with both thumbs touching the clay, put the thumb nails together until the first knuckles touch

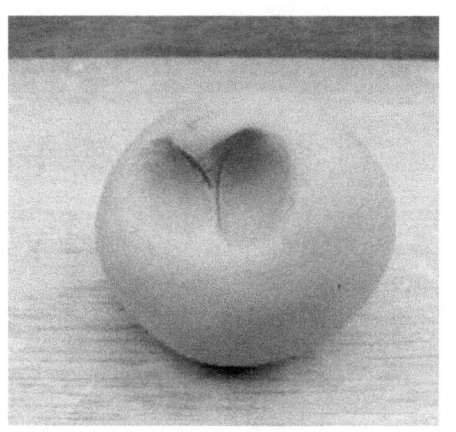

each other. Now press your thumbs firmly into the clay leaving two clear impressions like the ones in the picture.

Turn the clay round and put your thumbs back into the hole and press your thumbs into the clay again,

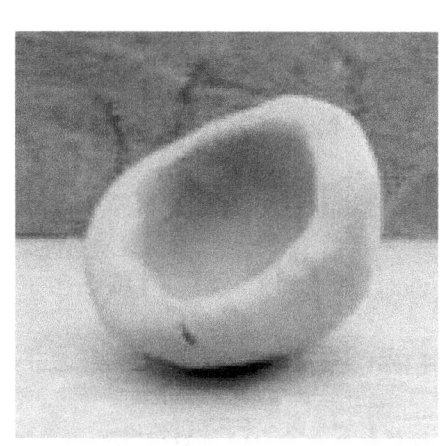

making the hole deeper. You can now use the pressure of your thumbs inside the pot against the fingers outside the pot to make the hole deeper and wider, turn the pot round as you gently squeeze the sides of the pot. At this point measure the diameter of your pot against the template on the worksheet, which is the diameter of the pot that you are aiming for. The overall effect can be likened to a half ball or the top of a mushroom.

Because we are making two thumb pots which have to be joined along the rims these rims need to be thick enough to form a substantial joint. Make sure that the rims are not too thin and that the thickness of the pot sides is carried through to the edge.

Make a second thumb pot.
Repeat the previous section to make a second, identical thumb pot, be sure that you follow the same process so that you will get the same result.

The next activity is to join the two pots along the rims, hold the two pots edge to edge to check that the diameters match and that there is sufficient clay to form a good seal at the joint.

Join two thumb pots.
One tip before we start the joining process, to give a better chance of matching the edges, is to hold each pot in your cupped hand and gently tap the edge on the work surface. This makes the edge level, smooth and slightly thicker making a good substantial surface ready for crosshatching.

With the point of the knife **crosshatch** both of the edges to be joined and create **slip** on both surfaces by rubbing the brush loaded with water across the crosshatch marks.

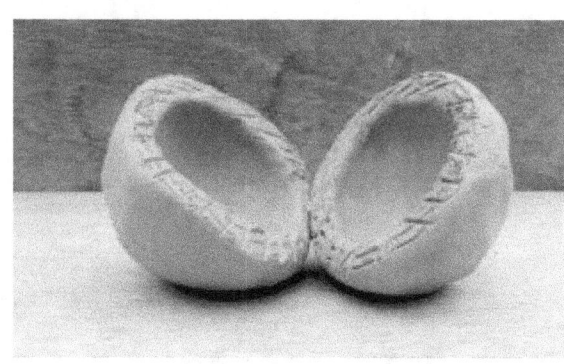

Hold one half of the body in the palm of your hand to support the edges and by holding the knife like a pencil you can use the sharp edge to score marks in the clay. Cut the marks into the surface in one direction, turning the half sphere around until the marks are around the complete circle. Reverse this process to make crosses on the whole surface as shown on the picture.

Repeat this process on the other half sphere before applying slip.

*The creation of **slip** is an important part of joining together two pieces of clay. The water from the brush is rubbed firmly into the clay surface until it turns light grey*

***Crosshatching** is one of the keys to joining two pieces of clay. It consists of the scoring the pieces in the areas to be joined. Use the point of the knife to mark clay.*

*The use of **pressure** is essential in successfully joining two pieces of clay when used in conjunction with crosshatching and slip.*

Creating slip on the crosshatch marks in this manner allows water to penetrate the crosshatch marks into

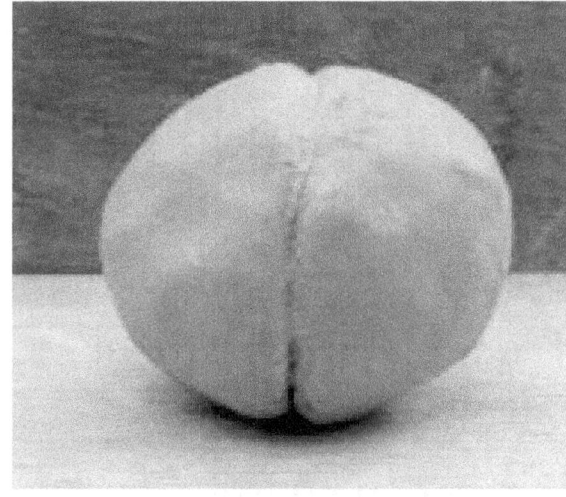

the clay surface forming a larger surface area for the water to soften and help to form the slip.

When you have prepared slip on both halves of the body hold one in each hand, bring the two prepared surfaces into contact and press them firmly together with a slight sliding motion across the surfaces to ensure that you get a good bond. The next part of the process is to seal and hide the joint. First, with the tip of your thumb or finger scrape clay from one half - sphere to the other alternating the strokes, one way then the other to give an even distribution. Use the flat surface of the knife blade like a spatula to further smooth and tidy the join.

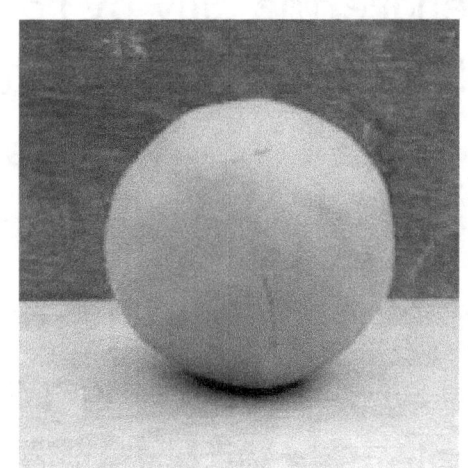

At this stage the body is a ball shaped piece of clay again, in fact it is actually a bubble of air surrounded by clay.

Finally take the hollow ball of clay in the palms of your hands and treat it like a solid ball by rolling it between your palms as you did in preparation, rolling it until it is smooth and free from blemishes. Final smoothing of the bubble of clay can be done on a plastic work surface if a really smooth surface is required.

Make and fit the head.

The head is formed by making another, smaller thumb pot which will be inverted and fixed to the top of the ball.

Prepare the clay by rolling it into a smooth ball which will be opened up with one thumb rather than both

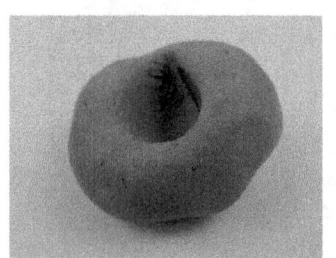

thumbs as the piece is smaller than the ones used for the body.

This time support the clay in the fingers of one hand while you make a single hole with your other thumb.

Continue to support the pot with your fingers and place your other thumb into the hole with your fingers on the outside of the pot. Gently press and squeeze the clay between fingers and thumb, turn the pot round slowly while continuing the squeezing action all the way round the periphery

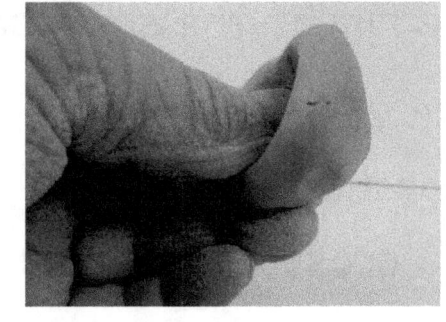

of the pot until it is the same diameter as the template on the worksheet.

Remember that you have to crosshatch the head to fix it to the body so try to keep the rim reasonably thick to ensure a stable joint is possible. Use the same technique used on the body to make the rim level and thicker, that is gently tap the rim on the work surface.

Make the body as deep as you can, it should be a hemi sphere when finished.

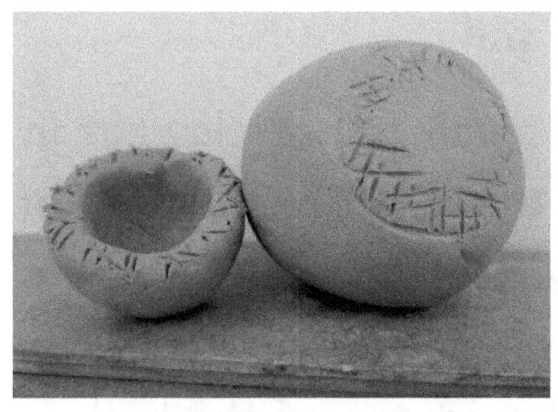

When the modelling of the head is completed place the rim on the body, and to mark the place where it is to be fitted draw a line gently around the rim onto the body.

Crosshatch a narrow area within the circle and round the rim of the small pot.

Use your slip brush and water to make slip on the crosshatch marks by rubbing the brush firmly into the crosshatch areas.

Press the rim of the head into the slip on the body, supporting the body in your palm like a ball while fixing the head with the other hand.

When the head is firmly in position you can cover the joint by smoothing clay from the head onto the body using the edge of your plastic knife.

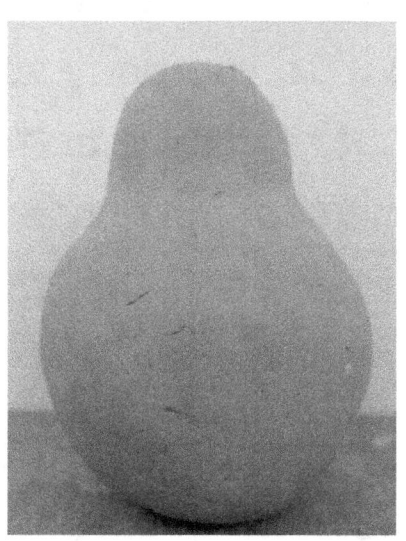

Smoothing the joint with the finger completes the action and serves to strengthen the joint.

Make and fit the feet and tail.

The feet are formed from a small ball of clay cut in

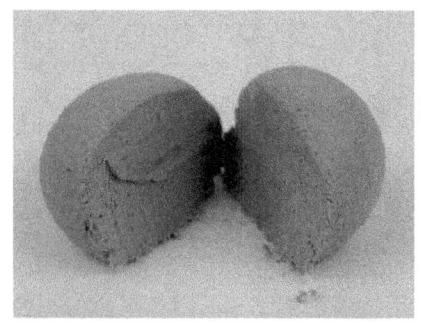

half and attached to the font of the body with slip. Roll the clay into a smooth ball, draw a line across the centre of the ball, check the position of the line and when you are satisfied that the line is in the middle cut the ball in half.

The pressure of cutting the clay in half makes the two halves flat on one side, this flattened area serves as the bottom of the feet and the flat edges where the clay was cut can be used, with slip, to attach the feet to the body. Apply slip with the brush and water to these flat sides and make two patches of slip on the body where the feet are to be attached. Press the feet firmly into position, again support the body like a ball to stop it squashing when the feet are being pressed on.

Making the tail consists of forming a ball into a cone shape.

First roll the clay into a smooth ball. Hold the ball between fingers and thumb of one hand and roll one end of the ball with enough pressure to form the clay into a fat point. Keep the point in the finger and thumb and press the rounded end onto the work surface to flatten it, this flat end fits onto the body with the pointed end making the tail.

Create a patch of slip using the brush and water on the body and rub the brush and water firmly on the flat end and press the two patches of slip together until the tail is attached. Smooth the joint using the tip of your finger to complete the bond. Check the picture which shows the feet and tail fixed in position.

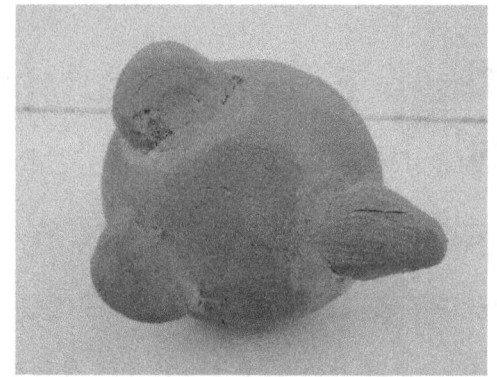

Make and fit the wings.

The wings are formed from a flattened ball of clay making a disc shape which is cut into two equal pieces.

Prepare the clay by rolling it between your palms to form a smooth ball. Use both hand to pat the ball flat forming a disc shape. Continue the patting until the disc is the diameter shown on the worksheet template.

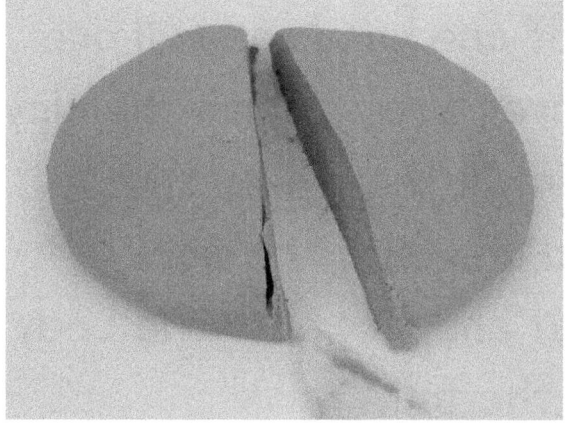

Draw a line across the diameter of the disc and when you are satisfied that the line is in the centre cut it in half.

Before you fix the wings into position place them on the model as shown on the picture.

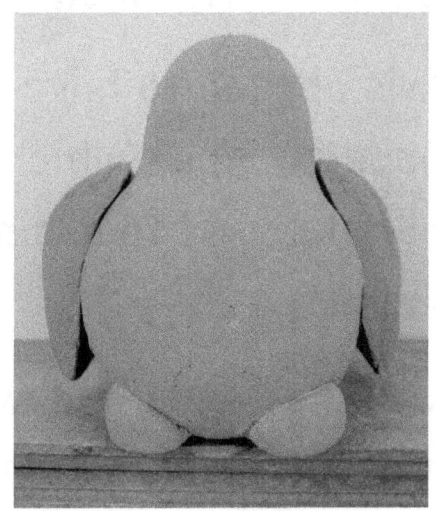

They will stay in position because the clay is wet, you can remove one wing and create a patch of slip on the side of the body with the brush and water.

Also create slip on the side of the wing where it will attach to the body. Press the wing firmly onto the body starting at the head end and press it into place leaving the lower end sticking out from the body.

Repeat this process with the other wing, check each side of the model to ensure the wing positions are identical.

Blend the top of each wing into the body with finger pressure.

Make the beak.

The beak is first made into a ball. Take the ball between the first finger and the thumb. Press the ball onto the work surface while at the same time squeezing it, the resultant shape is stuck with   slip between the eyes before modelling the shape as part of the modelling exercise.

Decorate the model.

Owls appear to have quite large eyes, they are dish shaped hollows which also help to collect sound to assist the owl's hearing.

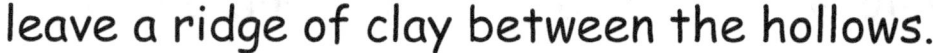

To make these hollows press the tips of your thumb in the position shown on the picture. This will leave a ridge of clay between the hollows.

Create slip on the ridge and on the flattened part of the beak and press the beak into position. Smooth the edges of the beak to blend it into the head and make the end into a slight hook shape with the point of your knife.

Use the wooden stick to make the eyes, make sure the stick pierces the clay to release steam if you intend to fire the model.

With the point/edge of your knife draw the radial lines from the eyes to simulate feathers.

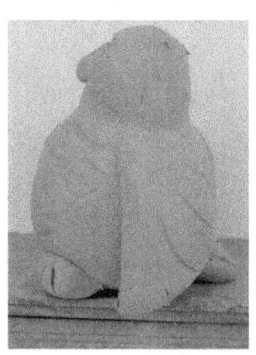

The feathers on the chest, wings, head and tail are created using the wooden stick. You can make clear lines by using the edge of

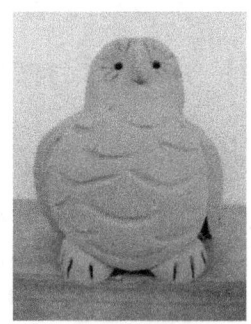

the stick rather than the point which tends to pluck the clay. Lay the last centimetre of the stick on the model where you want to draw the lines and slide the stick along the clay to make the marks.

Use the point of your knife to create the owl's claws, press the knife into the clay with the model standing on the work surface.

B & M Potterycrafts.

Double thumb pot owl. Worksheet.

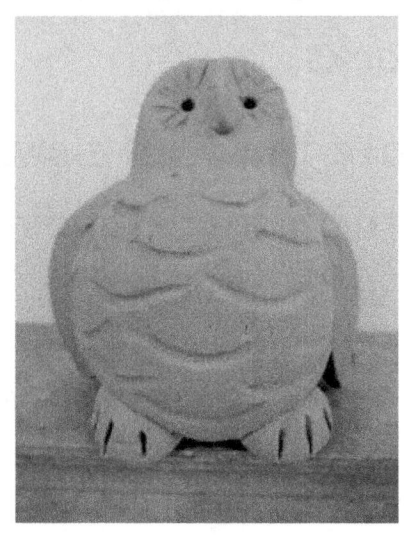 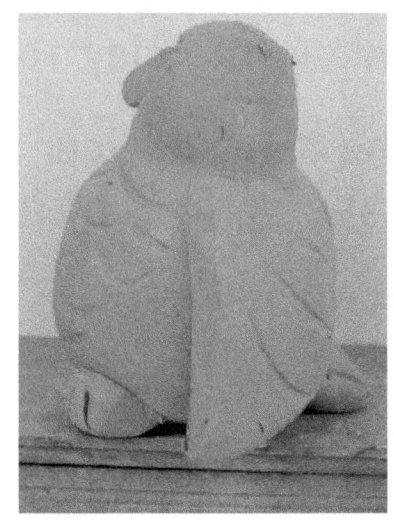

Clay.

Body. 100 grams x2.

7 cms.

Head. 30 grams.

4 cms.

Feet. 5/2 grams. Each.

Tail. 5 grams.

Wings. 50/2 grams each.

5.5 cms.

Beak. Small piece.

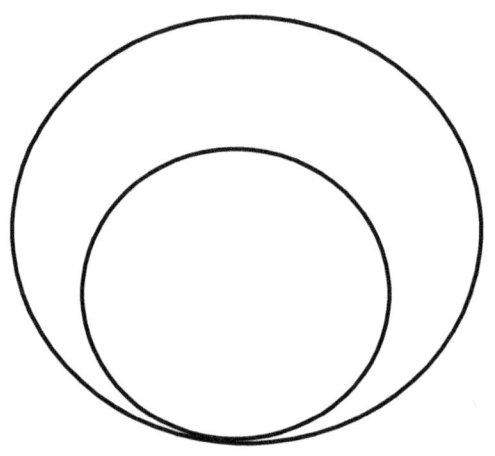

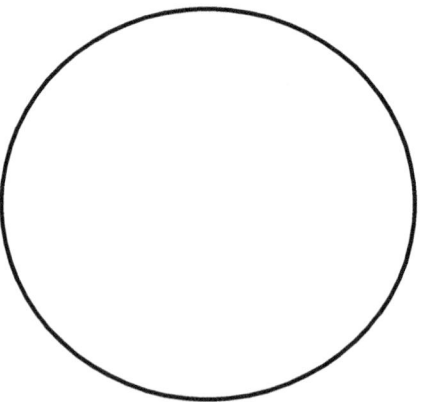

B & M Potterycrafts.

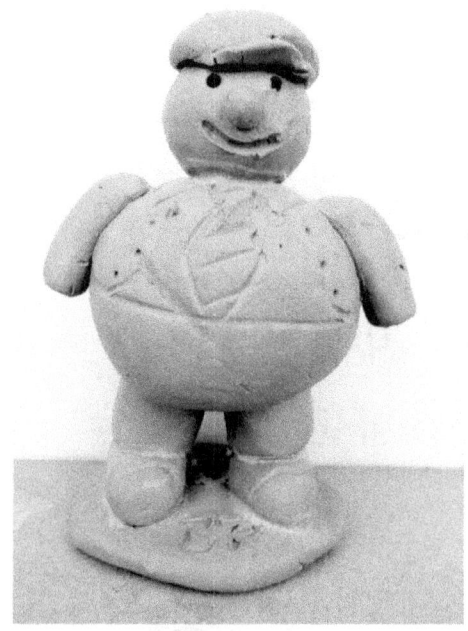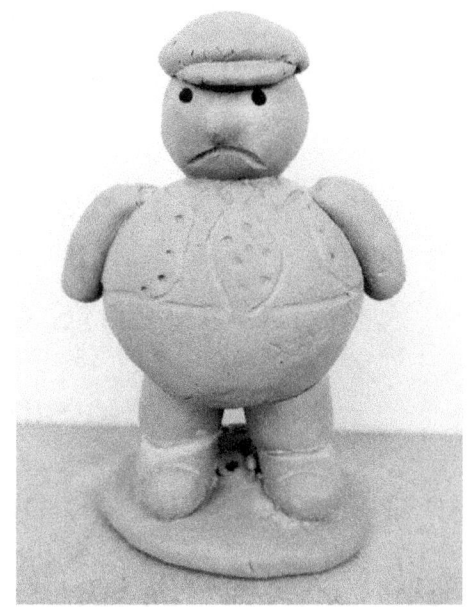

Clay modelling projects.

Double Thumb Pot.

Tweedle Dum and Tweedle Dee.

Create the model shown on this cover by following step by step, easy to understand, instructions supported by still photos at each stage.

Brian Rollins.

B & M Potterycrafts.

Tweedle Dum and Tweedle Dee.

Double Thumb Pot.

Contents and sequence.

Create a single thumb pot.

Make a second thumb pot.

Join two thumb pots.

Make and fit the head.

Make and fit the arms.

Make and fit the legs.

Make and fit the feet.

Make and fit the cap.

Detail the model.

Make the base and fit the model.

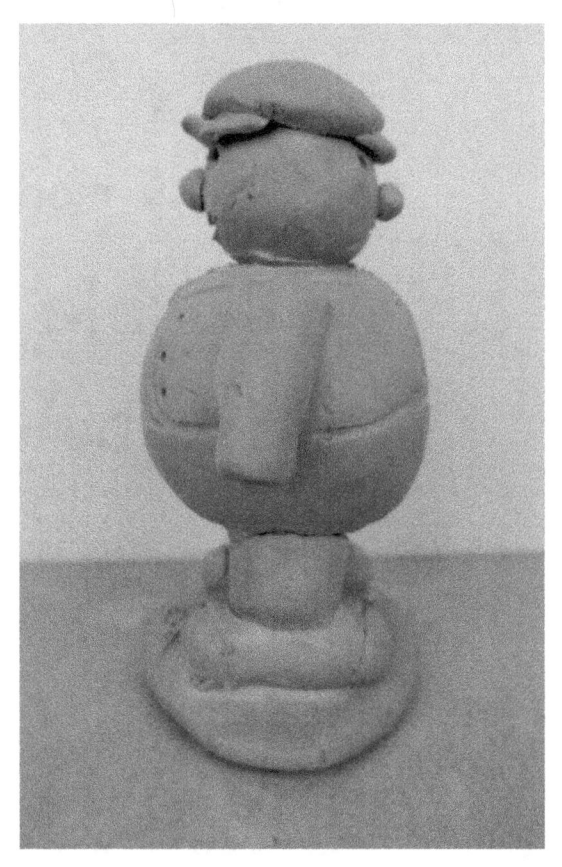

Worksheet.

Tweedle Dum and Tweedle Dee.

Create a single thumb pot.

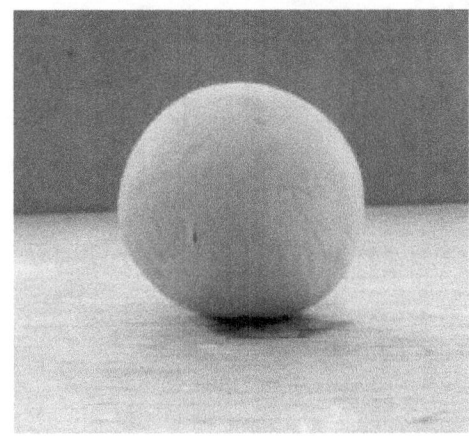 The first part in creating a thumb pot from a ball of clay is to ensure that the ball is round and smooth.

Roll the clay between the palms of your hands, exerting sufficient force to remove any lumps or bumps. Don't be tempted to take the easy route to smooth the clay by rolling it on the wooden work surface as this removes moisture from the clay and could make it too hard for modelling. Any creases or cracks can be smoothed using the fingers. Continue to roll the clay until the surface is smooth and the clay is the desired shape i.e. a ball shape.

The main reasons for this are that if the clay is not smooth before you start to stretch it any cracks will appear as a weakness and the clay will split at those points, to get round this problem check for cracks after each stage of the hollowing and stretching process, smooth out any cracks around the edge with pressure from your fingers.

Please note that if the clay isn't spherical before you start to form the pot you have little chance of finishing with a circular thumb pot.

To start the thumb pot hold the clay in the tips if the fingers of both hands with both thumbs touching the clay, put the thumb nails together until the first knuckles touch each other. Now press your thumbs firmly into the clay leaving two clear impressions like the ones in the picture.

Turn the clay round and put your thumbs back into the hole and press your thumbs into the clay again, making the hole deeper. You can now use the pressure of your thumbs inside the pot against the fingers outside the pot to make the hole deeper and wider, turn the pot round as you gently squeeze the sides of the pot. At this point measure the diameter of your pot against the template on the worksheet, which is the diameter of the pot that you are aiming for. The overall effect can be likened to a half ball or the top of a mushroom.

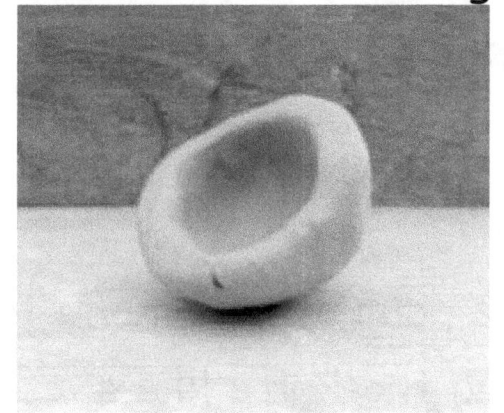

Because we are making two thumb pots which have to be joined along the rims these rims need to be thick enough to form a substantial joint. Make sure that the rims are not too thin and that the thickness of the pot sides is carried through to the edge.

Make a second thumb pot.

Repeat the previous section to make a second, identical thumb pot, be sure that you follow the same process so that you will get the same result.

The next activity is to join the two pots along the rims. Hold the two pots edge to edge to check that the diameters match and that there is sufficient clay to form a good seal at the joint.

Join two thumb pots.

One tip before we start the joining process, to give a better chance of matching the edges, hold each pot in your cupped hand and gently tap the edge on the work surface. This makes the edge level, smooth and slightly thicker making a level substantial surface ready for crosshatching.

With the point of the knife **crosshatch** both of the edges to be joined and create **slip** on both surfaces by rubbing the brush loaded with water across the crosshatch marks.

Hold one half of the body in the palm of your hand to support the edges and by holding the knife like a 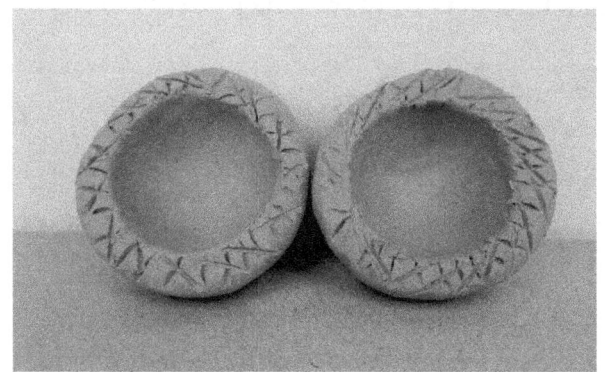 pencil you can use the sharp edge to score marks in the clay. Cut the marks into the surface in one direction, turning the half sphere around until the marks cover the complete circle. Reverse this process to make crosses on the whole surface as shown on the picture.

Repeat this process on the other half sphere before applying slip.

*The creation of **slip** is an important part of joining together two pieces of clay. The water from the brush is rubbed firmly into the clay surface until it turns light grey*

***Crosshatching** is one of the keys to joining two pieces of clay. It consists of the scoring the pieces in the areas to be joined. Use the point of the knife to mark clay.*

*The use of **pressure** is essential in successfully joining two pieces of clay when used in conjunction with crosshatching and slip.*

Creating slip on the crosshatch marks in this manner allows water to penetrate the crosshatch marks into the clay surface forming a larger surface area for the water to soften and help to form the slip.

Load your slip brush with water and rub it firmly over the crosshatched surface until you create sufficient slip. Using a stiff slip brush helps to break up the clay surface.

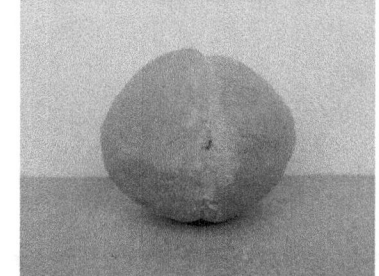

When you have prepared slip on both halves of the body hold one in each hand, bring the two prepared surfaces into contact and press them firmly together with a slight sliding and twisting motion across the surfaces to ensure that you get a good bond.

The next part of the process is to seal and hide the joint. First, with the tip of your thumb or finger scrape clay from one half - sphere to the other alternating the strokes, one way then the other to give an even distribution. Use the flat surface of the knife blade like a spatula to further smooth and tidy the join.

At this stage the body is a ball shaped piece of clay

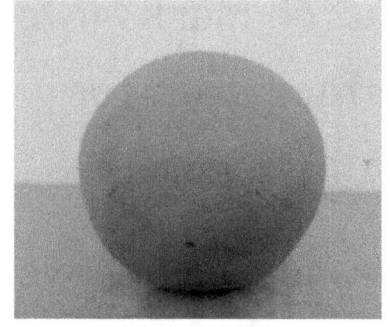 again, in fact it is actually a bubble of air surrounded by clay.

Finally take the hollow ball of clay in the palms of your hands and treat it like a solid ball by rolling it between your palms as you did in preparation, rolling it until it is smooth and free from blemishes. Final smoothing of the bubble of clay can be done on a plastic work surface if a really smooth surface is required.

Head to body.

Start by rolling the clay into a smooth ball and stand the body on one end .To attach the head to the body we need to make **crosshatch** marks and create **slip.** With the point of the plastic knife score '**#**' on 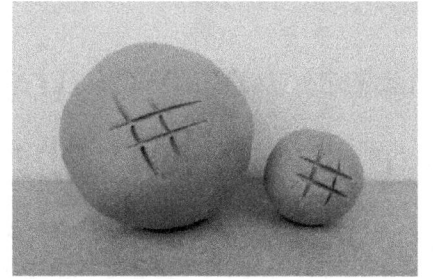 the top of the body and on the head where it is to be joined to the body. Dip the brush in water and firmly rub the brush and water across the '#' marks, the area will turn a lighter shade of grey, this material is **slip.** Finally **press** the head and body firmly together.

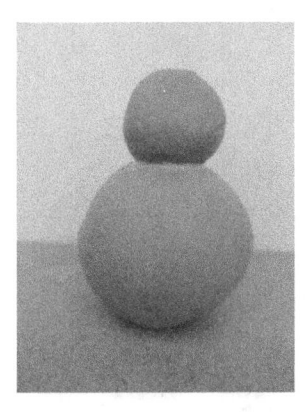

As the body is effectively a bubble of clay you should take care not to squash or distort the ball shape by holding the ball securely in your hand with fingers folded round the clay to support it while pressing the head into position.

Make and fit the arms.

The arms are made by first rolling the clay into a sausage shape the length shown on the worksheet.

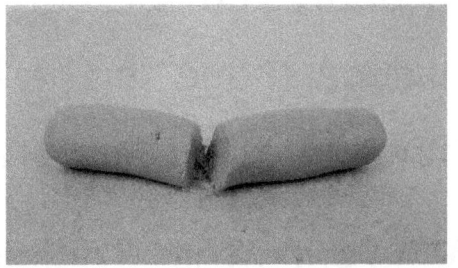

Mark the centre of the sausage with the point if the knife then cut it into two equal pieces.

Fit the arms to the body in the position shown on the picture. There is no need to crosshatch the pieces as there is quite a large surface of each arm in contact

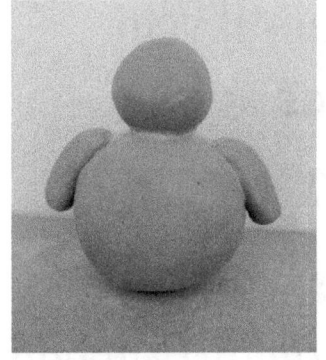

with the body and firm pressure will serve to attach the arms. Create slip on the body and along each arm and press the arms into place. Model the top of the arm to form the shoulder.

Make and fit the legs.

In order to support the body we will need to make quite sturdy legs.

The process we follow is to prepare the clay by making a smooth ball then a short fat sausage and finally cut the sausage in half to make the legs.

Roll the clay in the palms of your hands with enough pressure to make the clay round and smooth.

Secondly roll the ball across your palms to make a sausage shape to the length shown on the template.

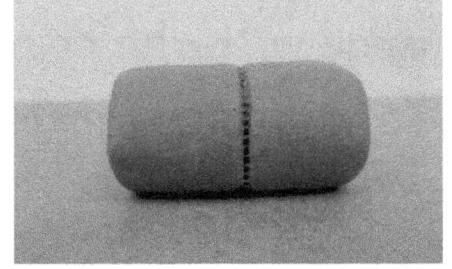

Make sure that the clay turns completely over on each roll. If you don't complete full turns the sausage shape will be flat.

Check the length against the template until you achieve the correct length. Tap the ends of the sausage shape to flatten it, readjust the length to match the template.

Mark the sausage across the middle and cut it in half when you are satisfied that the legs will be of equal length. Cutting the clay may flatten the legs a little, readjust the cylindrical shapes with finger pressure.

To ensure that the model stands erect both ends of

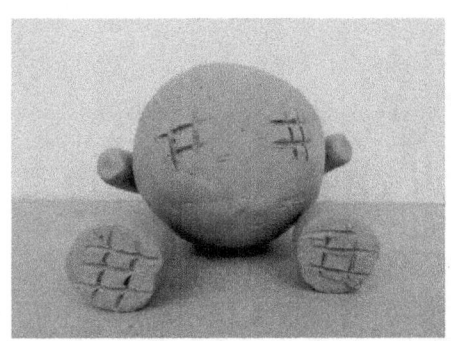

each leg needs to be flat. Tap each end gently on the work surface until they are flat. This may change the length which will need slight adjustment.

Crosshatch the underside of the body in two areas, in the positions shown in the picture and also crosshatch one end of each leg.

Create slip on all the crosshatch areas using the brush and water.

Support the body in the palm of your hand press each legs firmly into the slip on the body. Check that the figure will stand upright at this point just to allow you to adjust the positioning and length of the legs.

Lay the figure on his back until it is more stable, which will be after the feet are fitted.

Make and fit the feet.

To help make our model represent two characters we extend the feet to allow them to stick out on both sides.

The extra length is shown on the template so we make a sausage shape to match. Roll the clay to the length shown keeping the same thickness along the sausage shape.

With your fingers shape both ends of each piece to represent the front of shoes as shown on the picture.

Gently press your thumb along each shoe to make it slightly flat, crosshatch the top of both feet and the bottom of each leg. Create slip on these areas and finally press the feet firmly onto the legs. The model should stand upright at this point in the assembly.

Make and fit the cap.

The cap is made from two pieces of clay, the cap weighs 10 grams and the peak weighs 2 grams.

Roll the 10 gram piece into a ball and hold it in your palm, press the index finger of the other hand into the centre of the ball to make a shallow bowl shape.

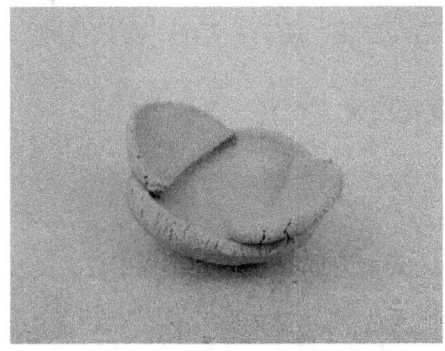 Make the bowl wider by shaping the inside with the tip of the finger. Continue this shaping until the bowl shape fits onto his head.

Make a ball with the second piece of clay and squash it flat with your thumb. Check that the disc is the correct size to make two peaks when it is cut in half.

Make two areas slip inside the cap and on the peaks, press the peaks into the cap and blend the pieces together to fit the shape of the head.

Create slip inside the cap and on top of the head, support the head while you press the cap into place.

Make and fit the base.

To complete the model and to enable it to stand erect we will attach it to the base.

Prepare the clay by rolling it into a ball, then squash it into a pancake shape big enough to fit both feet as shown in the picture the picture, try to ensure that the thickness is the same across the whole surface of the slab. If it is too thick in places the figure

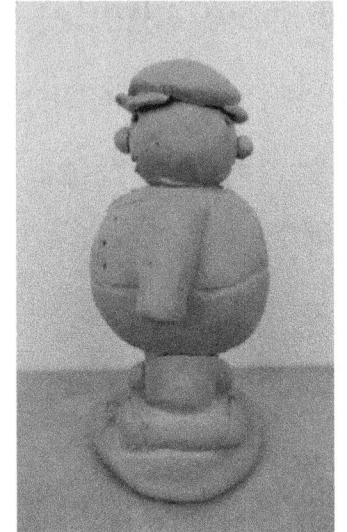 attached will be sloping. If it is too thin in parts the piece will be weak. Crosshatch the underside of the models **feet** and the base in the areas where the model will touch. Apply water with the brush to the model and the base creating slip on each piece. Finally press the model firmly down onto the base taking care not to distort the shape. Hold each leg and foot and press them separately into the slip on the base.

Decorate the model.

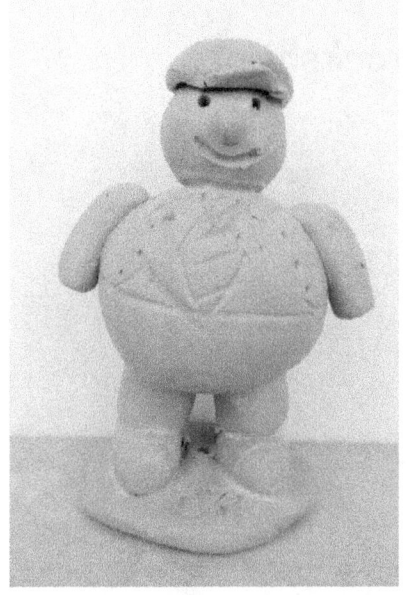 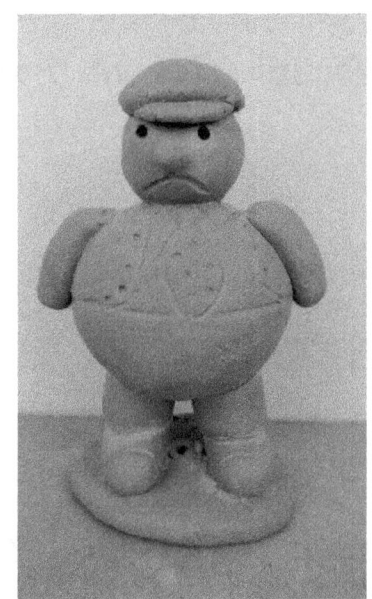

Add a small ball of clay to the front of the head at both sides to represent the nose. Use the pointed stick to make the eyes and the mouth.

I have decorated both sides with a shirt, tie and waistcoat showing the top of his trousers by a line around the middle. The toes of the shoes are also outlined, all done with the pointed stick or a sharp pencil.

Use your imagination to design your own figure.

B & M Potterycrafts.

Tweedle Dum and Tweedle Dee.

Double Thumb Pot. Worksheet.

Clay.

Body 80 grams x2.

Legs. 25 grams/2.

Feet. 15grams x2.

Arms. 15 grams/2

Hat. 10 grams.

Nose. Small piece.

Base. 60 grams.

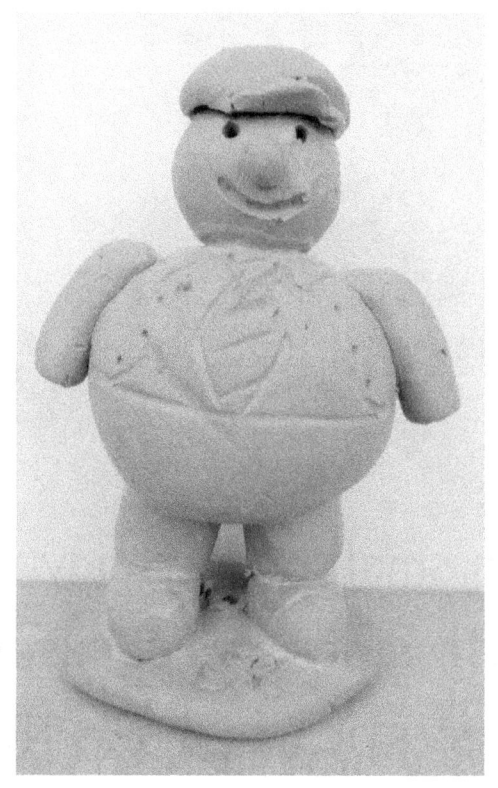

Legs

Feet.

Arms.

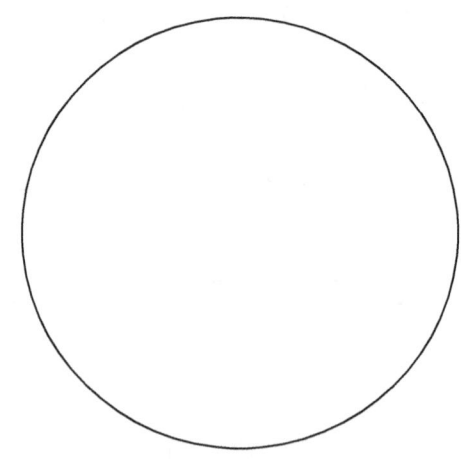

Body, 5.5 cms.

PS.

This model can be used in several educational ways.

First and obvious one is to teach students pottery and specifically how to create thumb pots.

Three dimensional art comes into the reckoning also literature and poetry to reinforce part of C S Lewis' Alice in Wonderland.

The model has also been used to indicate personal feelings. The model's features can be chosen to reflect Happiness and Sadness. It has been used this way with pupils having personal problems allowing them to express their feelings without direct answers.

Alternatively you can express your own feelings or even use the model to cheer yourself up by simply turning it to display 'Mr Happy' rather than 'Mr Sad'.

Brian.

www.ingramcontent.com/pod-product-compliance
Lightning Source LLC
Chambersburg PA
CBHW080709190526
45169CB00006B/2303